MOONWALKER

MOONWALKER

Adventures of a midnight mountaineer
By Alan Rowan

BackPage Press

BackPage Press

A catalogue record for this book is available from the British Library

ISBN: 9781909430174

Design and typeset by Freight Design
Illustrations by Dave Alexander
Printed and bound in Scotland by DS Smith Print Solutions

Thanks to Peter Macfarlane (www.petesy.co.uk)
for use of photography

www.backpagepress.co.uk
@BackPagePress

For Fergus

So many great mountains, so many great memories

Contents

Cast List

ALISON:

long-suffering wife who often suspects her husband is out wandering the hills, but when she does get told where he is she can't find a pen that works

FERGUS:

long-time hillwalking partner who will take on any mountain challenge but is reduced to a quivering wreck at the sight of over-priced bakery products

MALCOLM:

mountaineer, sailor and all-round adventurer, but definitely not a morning person

ELLEN:

wife of Malcolm, also with a passion for hills, but not so much that she appreciates a 5am phone call to reveal his whereabouts

SCOOP:

faithful canine partner of Malcolm, a little confused as to his role with sheep, not a fan of hats

ROBERT:

another occasional night adventurer, even if his mountain fashion tastes are suspiciously like those of Russell Brand's granddad

JIM:

sometime transport co-ordinator for Alan's long treks, but not always up to speed with popular lyrics

EVELYN:

a multi-coloured explosion of energy and enthusiasm but still ends up trailing behind the old guys

ALEX:

larger-than-life American visitor, tendency to mistake every rock he sees for a bird of prey

GILES:

literally a walking disaster, can turn the simplest trek into something more akin to The Poseidon Adventure

DEREK:

poster boy for the Munros but his numbers never add up

CRAWFORD AND REBECCA:

a couple with a real appetite for the outdoors – the mountains truly are food and drink to them

Close Encounters

IT IS 4AM AND I am sitting flat on my backside, slightly stunned, in a pitch-dark forest. I have just been head-butted by a tree.

It's an inauspicious start to what should have been a simple walk up through the woods on the way to climbing two mountains.

My night vision has tricked me. I left the car convinced I could see well enough to climb up the path through the dense forest ahead, certain that I did not need a torch. I was wrong. Not only could I not see the woods for the trees, I couldn't even see the trees and after only two or three steps one particular woodland inhabitant proved the point. Smack! I walked straight into the trunk.

My first thought is: What a bloody silly place to have a tree.
The second: What the hell am I doing in a coal-black forest at 4am?

Midnight. Four hours earlier.

I am sitting in the office of a national newspaper in Glasgow. For the past 12 hours, I have been helping run the sports desk. As usual, my job has been a constant battle to keep everything moving forwards: assigning writers their tasks, compiling a plan for tomorrow's sports pages; discussing these stories at an editorial conference; deciding which pictures and headlines to use and trying to read all the reporters' copy as it comes in.

All the while, the phone has not stopped ringing: reporters, photographers, readers, marketing departments and freelancers trying to sell a story. Pages are designed, revised, ripped up, redesigned, edited and proof-read. And every so often a hand grenade of ever-changing news is thrown at you.

The tension and stress builds by the minute. By deadline, you are so full of adrenaline that sleep is impossible. Some will go home for a late supper or a drink, some to watch television. But I have a compulsive desire to be in the mountains, and for most of the 1990s I had my sights set on the Munros, Scotland's 3,000 foot peaks. With 284 to conquer, I had decided to make the most of my time. Instead of joining the thousands of other walkers on the hills at weekends, I could have the wild places to myself by travelling there straight after finishing work around midnight.

On this night, as on so many others, I disappeared into a deserted office to appear minutes later, in true Clark Kent-style, changed from my suit into mountain gear.

The first time I did this, it drew comments of astonishment. Or to be more precise: "You're off your head." But, as time went by, a more frequent question was: "Where are you off to now?" Eventually, I would find one or two of the more curiously adventurous wanting to give it a try.

Minutes after my quick change in the office, I am on the familiar drive up the A82, the road from Glasgow into the West Highlands, heading for a better place. Forty minutes or so later, the massed orange glow of the big city has been left behind and I am driving alongside the banks of Loch Lomond.

Ben Lomond is the first major peak to show its profile against the night sky, the first promise of another great adventure. It is followed quickly by the Arrochar Alps and the Crianlarich peaks and, by the time mighty Ben Dorain rears into view, the mood has shifted from the stresses and worries of the newsroom into the anticipation of what lies ahead.

Some of the landmarks are like old friends. The Rannoch Rowan, for example, a lone tree which many years ago sprouted from a giant boulder, sits alone and aloof as you drive over the moor. I always wave as I pass, a salute from one lone Rannoch Rowan to another.

Then the 'Big Herdsman of Etive' comes into view, stately Buachaille Etive Mor, instantly recognisable to virtually every Scot from calendars and artwork even if they do not know it by name. It shepherds you into Glen Coe, past other iconic peaks as the road winds on to Fort William.

As I drive through the woods above Gairlochy, a massive white barn owl swoops silently out of the trees on the right, passing over the car and vanishing into the trees on the other side. Minutes later another one, even bigger, passes overhead, gone in a flash. At this rate, the next one will be the size of a polar bear.

I make my way to Clunes and then along to the Mile Dorcha – the Dark Mile. This is a stretch of road lined by huge beech trees which form a solid barrier, blocking most of the light. The road continues to the head of Loch Arkaig, deteriorating until grass is tickling the underside of the car. It must have more vomit stops per mile than any other road in the country. Take note Chris Rea – this is the road to hell.

I find the car park in a small clearing enclosed by trees. I switch off the Talking Heads tape that has accompanied me on my journey, and I turn off the engine. As always, I close my eyes now, for a few minutes of quiet contemplation before the hard work ahead. Then I get out of the car.

It's 3.30am. I am about to climb a mountain.

The night is clear and warm. The sky above the forest is awash with stars. The longer I gaze up, the more I believe I can see perfectly well with the light available.

However, the darkness at ground level is absolute, not a pinprick of light showing through the trees. Seconds later, I am on my backside. It's enough of a collision to knock me down, partly due to the surety with which I have been walking and partly because this is one of the last places I would expect to be mugged.

Now, after that sudden shock, I am wending my way upward at good speed. As I rise higher, slivers of moonlight start to ease their way through the gloom, enough to keep me from being the victim of another trunk collision. Down to my left, I can hear the constant swish of the as-yet invisible waters of the Allt Cam Bhealaich tumbling down towards the Eas-Chia-aig waterfalls.

Steeper and steeper into the wood, I begin to catch a glimpse of a pale, blue light filling the sky. Step by step, the blue grows in strength until all above the trees is a shimmering, brilliant azure, while behind me is only darkness.

The contrast is breathtaking, almost other-worldly. It's as if Steven Spielberg is directing my progress, arranging for the mother ship from *Close Encounters of the Third Kind* to hover over the forest, ready to spirit me out of the darkness and into the light.

Suddenly I'm standing at the edge of the forest, on the track up Gleann Cia-aig. I have walked from the dead of night into the sunshine of the start of another stunning day in a matter of minutes.

The light is so brilliant that the track ahead takes on the appearance of a white ribbon running parallel with the river. The fragility of the early-morning light is highlighted when the track disappears into a tree-lined section, a dark tunnel which reminds me of the true time of day.

This leads to a small and increasingly unstable bridge over the river, just as the walls pinning in the waters begin to steepen. Every visit seems to find the bridge with fewer planks; a few more years and there may just be the outline skeleton sitting there.

The path now vanishes into a sea of yellow vegetation which involves a lot of hopping from foot to foot to avoid water-filled holes, little streams and patches of bog. The twin humps of the two Munro peaks are now firmly in the line of sight.

Soon I pick up a good path which runs along the side of Sron a'Choire Ghairbh and leads up to the pass between the hills, the Cam Bhealaich. From this lofty point, I look down on Loch Lochy and watch the tiny cars zipping along the road, thousands of feet below.

A grassy, stepped path leads to the cairn on Sron a'Choire Ghairbh, and the revealing of a more spectacular and shapely character to the mountain. Then it's back to the col for a refreshments stop, before the weary push up to Meall na Teanga. The summit view is a delight, likewise the short, high-level ridge leading to the next peak, Meall Coire Lochain, which looks down on a dark little loch, cradled in the steep-sided corrie bowl like an inkwell filled to the brim, sitting in splendid isolation.

It is around 11am when I get back to the car park, which now has a few other inhabitants, most preparing to embark on the walk I've just completed.

By the time my colleagues at the newspaper have risen and are preparing for lunch, I have had breakfast thousands of feet further up and am driving back to arrive at work with them.

In the 15 hours since we parted, I have made an 11-hour round trip, climbed two mountains and not slept a wink.

1
Treig and Intrigue

MY NAME IS ALAN and I'm an alpaholic. I am addicted to mountains. I need them. I have to get out at least once a fortnight. If I don't, I get bad-tempered, fidgety and my concentration starts to wander. All I can think about is my next fix.

For the last 20 years or so, the priority every week has been to climb a hill. No sooner has it been conquered than the planning must start for the next one. And the next. And the next.

It consumes you piece by piece, like a snake swallowing its tail. The more I did, the more I wanted – no, needed – to do. The planning became just as important as the climbing, hours spent working out the logistics of getting there, the best route up, both aesthetical and practical, and exactly how much would be too much to take on.

Which is why I was now slogging my way up a rising ramp of grass and scattered boulders towards two peaks in the wild region east of Fort William as the morning light was starting to filter through.

I should have been in bed, asleep, recovering from a hard day at the office. Instead, here I was, heading for the twin pyramids of Stob a'Choire Mheadhoin and Stob Coire Easain. It was not yet 4am and this was my first night assault on the Munros.

I had already racked up 53 peaks in just over a year in my quest to do the Munros. Most of these had been done with my buddies Fergus and Malcolm, but I just could not get enough and was becoming frustrated at the thought of all these hills that were outside our usual time limits. When I pitched the idea of overnight climbs to the pair of them, I was met with: "Yeah, right." That was the end of the conversation. They thought my proposal was just a whim.

But once an idea forms in my head, it is hard to shift. At the very least, it would be worth experimenting. One trip could not hurt.

So here I was striding up a three-mile rising ridge, alone. My body was still adjusting to this alien experience as I pushed on. The first hour of any climb is always tough as your body fights to adjust to the sudden shock. When you are doing it before dawn, it seems doubly hard.

Your legs feel like they have lead weights attached. Your breathing is heavy. Your head is telling you that this is wrong, wrong, wrong. And yet you move on step by step, making what is often referred to as controlled progression. That is just a fancy way of saying it's a slog.

There is no path. I weave in and out of rocky outcrops and undulating grassy terrain to find the best line. The only thing that matters is the next horizon. It is like an uphill slalom. All this time the morning is rising with me, changing the colours of the terrain with every step.

Then there is the magic moment when I break the back of the climb. The gradient eases and the ground becomes firmer. I move towards my target faster, like a rocket jettisoning its heavy, bottom section. And finally there is the feeling of elation when the summit is in sight. The thought that I still have to cover the same distance to get home hardly ever figures. It is all about the moment.

I am lying out above 3,000 feet in the early-morning sunshine. My wife, Alison, and daughters, Claire and Lucy, are blissfully unaware of where I am and what I have been doing. It is not a case of telling lies, more a sin of omission. There is no point telling them in advance what I am planning to do, no point in them having a sleepless night worrying about me.

They have often played second fiddle to my obsession. They also know that life is much sweeter this way. Better a happy, satisfied husband and father most of the week than a grumpy one all of the week. Besides, Superman is not the only one who needs a fortress of solitude. This was my secret, my me-time, a regular slot to chat with myself and find solutions to any troubles.

As for work? Well, I've always regarded it as merely a means to support my hobby. I take pride in doing my job well but it is a job, not a lifestyle. One should work to live, not live to work. I always felt immense sadness when I heard colleagues say they would not know what to do with themselves if they did not work.

I was lucky with my career. I worked for a national newspaper in Glasgow, which meant doing backshift for most of the last 20 years. Starting times ranged from 2.30pm to 7.30pm, finishing times from 9.30pm to 3am, and the rolling rota was over six days so that some weeks you were off Mondays, some Tuesdays, and so on. The only day I did not have to work was Saturday, which was sacrosanct. I never walked or climbed on a Saturday. That was a day for the family.

My home is on the east coast and, as Alison and my girls were settled there, I lived in Glasgow during working spells and returned home for my days off. It was unusual to have to work five days straight through, but sometimes you could have five days off in a row.

I spent down time between working by going to the cinema, meeting friends for lunch and wandering around book stores, but I needed to keep fit. I am not a fan of gyms. It had to be the outdoors. But it is hard to find team sports taking place during the day, so it had to be something I could do solo.

I started taking my lunch in the great outdoors. I would hike for a couple of hours, find a spot and then settle down for a bite to eat and some sunbathing. It would be the ideal antidote to the pressures of the office.

From simple beginnings come great things. The need to get out grew, the targets became bigger, more elusive, more prized. Mountains would become my sport and my fulfilment.

This was my personal triumph, something that set me apart from my colleagues. A round of golf or a walk in the park was often the limit for many of them, no six, seven or eight hours of constant uphill movement in the middle of the night.

Gazing out of the office windows on a lovely day, it was easy to imagine myself scaling a mountain, but when the dark cloak of night had descended and the weariness of the day had set in, that was the real test. The hardest part of going climbing at night was winning the battle of will with a body that naturally wanted to shut down. And it was a constant fight. Every time I went out I had this inner struggle, but most of the time I won.

The ability to turn my back on my natural instincts would lead to this moment, the struggle up a faraway slope in the middle of the night.

The first two forays into nocturnal walking gave me the ideal grounding for the many trips that would lie ahead. The first went like clockwork. The weather was superb, the timings were spot on and it was a huge success. The second was exactly the opposite. The clinging cloud never lifted, the visibility was non-existent and it was not a particularly pleasurable night out. The experience of both sides of the coin was to prove invaluable. When I set out for the Easains, the mountains were still shedding their winter garb, and the temperature was rising by the day. But that was only one consideration in my choice of day and hill.

I did not want to have to travel too far the first time. I had no idea how I would react to the lack of sleep and the journey, no idea how I would fare tackling a 3,000-feet plus climb in the middle of the night when I would normally be sleeping, and no idea how I would manage the drive back and then do a long shift at work.

The hills had to be sufficiently far away. There was no point in an overnight journey and climb to a peak I could do comfortably during any normal day. Also, if I was going to make a long journey, I would be as well climbing a couple of peaks rather than just one.

The twin peaks which rise above Loch Treig were perfect. They are similar in appearance and shape and are joined together by a high bealach. The legendary mountaineer Hamish Brown once jokingly referred to them as This Yin and That Yin, a sobriquet which has stuck.

To reach the starting point meant making the familiar 100-plus mile run up the A82 to Fort William and then on to Spean Bridge. From there I would take the A86 east before turning down the narrow public road to Fersit, which sits on the line of the West Highland Railway.

The drive time would be about three hours. I reckoned if I left work at midnight, I would be there for about 3am. That would give me time enough for a nap if required before climbing the hills and returning with time to spare for a 5pm start in the office.

I packed a sleeping bag and travel pillow, and made sure I had plenty of energy snacks and fruit. I also had a caffeine lake with me, cans of Coke in the car for the journey back and a flask of coffee. My route had been posted with several colleagues – which they noted with some disbelief – and I was clear for take-off.

Travelling long distances at night is usually a case of quiet roads and whispered radio voices. I enjoy driving, and although there is not much to see on the outward journey, there is the anticipation of the return when everything you have only imagined in the darkness will become clear. In the years that followed I found myself catching up on whole back catalogues of music I had missed.

If the weather was fine and it was a clear night, I counted down the journey by ticking off the dark shapes of the familiar landmarks along the route. On overcast nights with no visibility above a few hundred feet, I felt I was in a road movie, headlights picking the way through an unseen landscape and, if the heavens opened, the music was turned up to drown out the drumming on the roof.

On my first night the sky was clear, and my mood was euphoric. Four days earlier I had finally seen Dundee United, my team, win the Scottish Cup, a fitting reward after six previous failed attempts, and I was still on a high.

My drive progressed with a selection of mellow and wild music. Talking Heads were a constant companion and John Martyn kept me chilled after the radio contact in the first part of the journey was lost; then a bit of Led Zep and other heavy metal in the latter stages to get me pumped up for the task ahead. Stairway to Heaven? I could only hope. But as I passed through Spean Bridge and started looking for the turn-off for the few miles down to Fersit, the music was switched off. I always prefer a few moments of silence before the hard work starts.

The twisting, narrow road south to the head of Loch Treig is only a couple of miles long but it passes over an old bridge and then through beautifully wooded areas before ending at a small quarry where I parked. It was down this quiet road that Hitler's right-hand man Rudolf Hess was held for a spell after his wartime flight to Scotland in 1941.

Hess had crash-landed in a field near East Kilbride, supposedly while flying in to make a peace offer, and was moved around the country. One of his 'holiday' homes while in Scotland was Inverlair Lodge, which is tucked in just off the road to the left. It is always disappointing to tell people that to see the house where Hess was held, you have to take a first left: it would be much better if it was third Reich.

There was no sign of any life as I stopped at the edge of An Dubh Lochan, 'the little black loch'. The moonlight shimmering on the dark water had turned the scene into a beautifully stark, black-and-white image. I had been weary in the latter stages of the drive but, at 3.15am with the light reflecting brilliantly off the still water and a cacophony of newly roused birds starting to pierce the silence, sleep was out of the question. The adrenaline was pumping.

When solo, it takes just five minutes from arrival at the destination to actually setting off. A few moments of quiet contemplation, eyes shut and head on the seat rest, is all that is required.

With the help of my head torch, a short walk over a level, grassy meadow took me over the line of an old mining tramway and then I rose on to the broad ridge for the ascent. With the early rising light starting to pick out the way, I was soon on steeper ground at Meall Cian Dearg, a minor rocky section on the way to my first Munro of the day, Stob a'Choire Mheadhoin.

Off to my left were the remains of the massive cornices that had smothered the cliff walls above Loch Treig but which were now cracking and slewing off in great slabs, ready to collapse down the mountainside, eventually to melt into the water and complete the wet fall to earth which began months before.

By 6.30am I was on the stony top of Stob a'Choire Mheadhoin, 'the peak of the middle corrie', to be greeted by a fluttering red flag planted in the summit cairn. My first nocturnal Munro and the flags were out to salute my achievement. Treig Heil, if you like.

Stob Coire Easain is one of the few mountains whose English translation – 'the peak of the corrie of the little cascade' – trumps the beauty of its Gaelic name. It is only about half a mile further on, a steep half-hour walk over stony terrain, up a graceful, curving ridge with the snow lines of the cornice providing a metaphorical handrail.

With the steepness of the ascent, the summit cairn cannot be seen from below, and it was here that I had my first taste of the mind playing tricks, a phenomenon that was to become a recurring feature of walking in the wee, small hours. As I approached the final push, a huge bank of snow stood in front of me, a giant lip in front of a cairn which I still could not see.

I stopped. All I could see was snow. Maybe there wasn't any more ground ahead. I could step over this snow and plummet into thousands of feet of thin air.

No, this was daft. Of course there was solid ground – I had seen the cairn from the other peak. Pushing my doubts aside, I stepped in and then over the snow. I was standing at the second summit.

With a snow wall all around the cairn, the crown of this peak was like an eyrie, a beautiful spot for breakfast. Sitting there at 7am with the snow-capped Grey Corries and the Nevis Range prominent in the morning sunshine, I wondered why anyone would want to climb at any other time. Everybody else was out of step, not me.

As I was sitting back at the car, basking in the glow of self-satisfaction, my socks off as I massaged my weary feet, another vehicle drew up. After a few minutes the driver got out, all kitted out for a day in the hills, and strolled over to where I was sitting.

"Are you going up the hills?" he asked.

"No, I've already been up."

It was the first time I had seen that look, a combination of puzzlement and almost fear. He retreated to his car. It was another first, but it would not be the last.

My journey back to Glasgow was slow, with constant pit stops for caffeine and snacks and, at one point, a nap. The sun was out, it was a glorious day and the Munro hotspots were packed with cars and walkers preparing to start their day. The night shift had finished, the day shift was beginning.

I managed to get through my shift at work without dozing off. The nocturnal adventure had been a resounding success. My hunch had paid off. This was the way I would conquer the Munros.

The chance of a second bite at the cherry did not arise for another six weeks. During this spell I had managed to tick off another 20 Munros in just six outings, including a big weekend away, taking my total up to 75. I was on a roll, and I decided to keep it going by upping the ante on my next night fling.

I was going to head into the Mamores to try to do at least three, maybe more. The journey to the village of Kinlochleven takes just a couple of hours and, being early July, the light should have been good enough for a very early start. The last three outings had been in exceptionally fine weather, and the forecast for this day looked like being the same again.

The Mamores are a chain of mountains to the south of Ben Nevis and it is possible to do all 10 Munros there in one big round. It is a long day, certainly too much if you factor in the car journey and lack of sleep, but I figured that with the good tracks into these hills and a superb path network, I could get going in the dark and conquer a few at least. But, to paraphrase Burns, the best-laid schemes o' mice an' madmen gang aft a-gley.

It had been a good night at work. At the 1994 World Cup, Bulgaria had pulled off a massive shock by beating Germany 2-1 and the buzz you get from a genuinely thrilling football match was still reverberating in my head as I headed off into the night. Rather than start from sea level, I parked at the Mamore Lodge hotel, a few hundred feet higher up, a nice wee starter for the day. It would be a slightly longer walk from there but I had reckoned trading distance for a small height gain was worth it. By 2.30am I was on the move, heading north on a good track into Coire na Ba, 'the corrie of the cattle'.

My first objective was to reach the col between Stob Coire a'Chairn and Na Gruagaichean. Then I would head south-east on to the twin summits, before continuing on the main ridge round to Binnein Mor, down one of its long arms and over to Binnein Beag and then sweep up Sgurr Eilde Mor on the way out. It was ambitious for a night walk but I did not foresee any difficulties. But I had been banking on the thick, early morning cloud blowing away sooner rather than later. And it was not showing any sign of doing so.

The damp was creeping through my layers and the ferns and grasses that had been soaking into my feet and legs earlier had left a wet overcoat that was not shifting as I plodded upwards on a muddy path into the corrie with nothing to see ahead of me. I was walking in a strange, half-lit gloom that was more akin to a day in December than July.

On my left was the massive Am Bodach, all dark cliffs and slashed gullies with white sheets of water roaring and tumbling down out of the greyness, moisture oozing and dripping from every orifice. It is a mountain with the power to intimidate, a brute looming threateningly out of the mist with seemingly no chinks in its armour. Somewhere up ahead on my right, smothered under the wall of cloud, were the twin summits of Na Gruagaichean but for now all I could see was long, wet grass in the limited horizon available.

An unexpected flash of colour briefly broke the monotony; a lone foxglove off to the right, cerise bells being pulled down by the weight of the water. Then it was back to the green and the grey as the flower was swallowed by the cloud and I continued upwards to my first target.

Eventually the path's long, contorted approach led me over the steep slopes which pulled up to the col, but there was still no sign of the cloud dispersing. In mornings like these, the myth of the silence and solitude of the great outdoors is easily dispelled. With the stillness around me, every movement of water sounded like a raging torrent. The sound of each laboured step seemed to be amplified tenfold, even above the heavy breathing of a man who realised that he should really be at home, tucked up in bed like every other sane human being. It ought to be all beautiful views bathed in yellow and orange light, not some trudge up the rock-strewn gloom of Mount Anywhere.

This was not pleasure. This was revenge for the smugness of my last outing. It was as if some greater power was saying: "That'll teach you."

The first of the two towers of Na Gruagaichean loomed. It is an impressive lump of rock, even more so when you make your way down the other side among lots of loose earth and rock to be confronted with the equally steep pull up its twin, the main summit.

According to Gaelic legend, this mountain got its name, which translates as 'The Damsels', from two young ladies who met a hunter on these slopes and gave him a hunting dog. There were no strange women here today, however, and the only dog was the climb.

I was shuffling along like a zombie; this was indeed the night of the living dead. I needed a view to lift the spirits but, by the time I reached the boulder field at the summit, I was beaten. No sign of anything ahead, no sign of anything behind. My heart was not in this any more. I just wanted to get back to the car. And that probably led to what happened next.

What should have been a simple walk over to the next peak became a confused effort in the mist and boulders. I ended up dropping down too low off the ridge and then the compass went crazy.

I suddenly had no true idea of exactly where I was. I was wandering around at 6am on a heather and boulder clad slope, having lost my bearings and with no visibility. I had lost the plot.

I knew the bulk of Binnein Mor was somewhere above me. That was logical, but logic seemed to be going out of the window.

After about half an hour of aimless and weary movement, I decided enough was enough. Heading down the corrie would take me out of the cloud and hopefully give me some idea of my whereabouts.

After a battle to get through some sofa-size boulders, real ankle snappers, I could see a path below.

At last I knew where I was. I could have resumed the walk from here – Binnein Mor was back up the ridge on my left – but I did not have the mental strength for any more. I just wanted to lie down and sleep. It was time to accept defeat and head down from the hills.

The cloud lifted when I was driving back down the road and it turned into a beautiful day. I could have been dancing round these peaks had I started walking at a sensible time. I was deflated. This night had been a disaster, and I was not sure I could handle night walking if the weather was unfavourable. I would either have to toughen up or forget this whole idea.

2
Going Tonto

IT COULD HAVE BEEN a scene from the dawn of time. Two tiny figures standing like statues high on a mountain ridge, watching in awe as the sun rises. Fingers of gold were shooting out, creating a light show of spokes in a wheel while the centre of the attraction was still hidden behind the bulky, dark monolith of Ben Nevis. How many times have humans stood transfixed by this sight over the years?

There is something so simple and yet so profoundly stunning about a sunrise. But you can only enjoy the dawning of a new day if you are there. You cannot rely on video replays.

The spectacular 3.30am light show was just the tonic for Malcolm and I after a punishing climb to the ridge of Mullach nan Coirean. I had persuaded a reluctant Malcolm that he should join me on a journey into darkness. My tales of Loch Treig had provided enough of a hook to catch his interest. Now I could only hope that the beauty of the dawn and the colours of the mountains at this time of day would reel him in.

So far, though, all we had experienced was the sweat and pain of a constant struggle through a dark forest and then a seemingly vertical grass slope with muddy steps.

The rising sun changed all that. It appeared almost right on cue, just as Malcolm was starting to have thoughts of violence against whoever had persuaded him to miss a night's sleep to climb a mountain.

It changed the mood, and it changed the pace like a direct shot of adrenaline to the heart. Suddenly there was no tiredness, no complaints. There was sunshine and joy.

I confess I was surprised when Malcolm caved in to my sales pitch. I was also delighted. I am quite content to walk on my own. There is a big difference between being lonely and being alone. Sometimes being alone is just what the doctor ordered. There are always moments during the walk when you see something so stunning that you wish someone was there to share it with. But that is not loneliness, just a realisation that what you are doing is right for you. In any case, if you can't stand your own company, why would you think it is fair to inflict it on anyone else?

However, it is good to have the option of decent company – and someone else to do the driving is always welcome.

The downside to this, though, was Malcolm's notorious track record with cars. I am sure that if you added up the amount he spent on cars during his lifetime you could not even put a down payment on a set of tyres for a BMW.

This time he had excelled himself. He had bought a car for £50 from a guy called Tonto. This transaction caused much hilarity when he proudly broke the news to his colleagues at work.

"You bought a car for £50?"

"No, he bought a car for £50 from a guy called Tonto."

"I wasn't aware that there were many reputable Apache car dealers in Scotland."

"That's right. I'm sure that Custer's Last Stand was the culmination of a long-running dispute over a wagon-wheel warranty."

"Is there not a Sitting Bull Motors out in Mount Vernon?"

"No, that's an Arnold Clark."

"Is it a Grand Cherokee you've bought?"

"Do you have to shout Geronimo when you jump into it?"

I'm still not sure what make of car it was. Some kind of hybrid, but not in a good way.

"Are you sure this is going to be okay?" I asked while we still had a chance to abandon this latest aberration and travel in my car.

"It's fine. Just one wee problem – I've only got second and fourth gears."

In Malcolm's world of cars, this was only a minor problem. I have always been fascinated to find out what constitutes a major problem for him. Even the time his car was splitting while travelling on the M8, the back end weaving from lane to lane, did not seem to disturb him. The solution to the present problem was an expandable luggage holder wound several times round and over the gear stick.

"We get it going, I put it in second, then tighten the expander round the gear stick to stop it jumping out of gear. When the revs are up, I lift the expander, ram the gear stick into fourth, and then tighten the expander again. It works okay."

"What about changing down?"

He looked at me as if it was a stupid question. "Just reverse the whole process. Piece of piss. I've been driving around like this for weeks."

Being driven anywhere by Malcolm was an experience. I remember being fascinated by his Border Collie, Scoop, sitting on the back seat with his claws dug into the seat.

"What's up with him?" I asked.

"Oh, he learned that as a pup. He was sitting on the back seat when I hammered on the brakes and he ended up on the dashboard. Clung on like that ever since."

And he did.

Unlike Scoop, I didn't have claws, but maybe because of the two-hand gear shuffle he had to employ, Malcolm was keeping his speed down and it was a surprisingly pleasant and unusually uneventful drive up to Glen Coe.

As we drove over the bridge at Ballachulish, things changed. Malcolm decided he needed a smoke, despite us being only 20 minutes or so from our destination. We stopped in a layby just beyond the bridge and he had his ciggie. The silence was absolute. Straight ahead, across the water, were the moonlit mountains of Ardgour and behind us the metal frame of the bridge seemed to be glowing white-hot. Unfortunately the car had obviously chosen this moment to have a break as well because when we got back in and tried to start it – nothing.

There we were around 1.30am, not another car on the road, pushing this heap along the A82. Pushing a car is always hard work. Pushing it while wearing full mountain gear is doubly hard work – at this rate we would be knackered before we got anywhere near a mountain.

It was only a couple of minutes but it seemed like an eternity. There was still no sign of life. Much more of this and there would be no signs of life from us either. But after a couple of miles we hit a downhill stretch, and it was at this point the car decided to wake up. Suddenly, there was a huge bang then everything in the car lit up, the engine started roaring and the Ride of Frankenstein took off faster, it seemed, than it had done all the way up from Glasgow. I could have sworn that I had seen a lightning bolt hit the car and heard Malcolm shouting: "It's alive, it's alive!"

Malcolm grabbed the wheel while I clung to the wide-open front passenger door, running alongside, in a bid to jump into the car. After three or four attempts and a few near things I managed to scramble in.

I was struggling for breath but I did manage to get out: "Your. Car. Is. A. Total. Bastard."

The shock of the breakdown seemed to have had an effect on both Malcolm and the car, and we were now back at normal Malc-speed, taking corners on the single track road in Glen Nevis at about 30mph faster than we had on the empty, open road earlier.

When I pointed this out in a slightly terrified way, he said: "We need to keep the speed up now. Don't want it giving up the ghost again."

It was with great relief that we arrived at our stopping point at the old cottage at Achriabhach. We sat for a moment. It seemed there was nothing to say. It was time to put the drive and push behind us and set up for the mountain.

However, a quick change of clothes was not easy. "Your boot is stuck," I told Malcolm.

"Ah, that could be because there was cement dripping on to it the other day while I was working on the boat. Maybe it's affected the hinges."

The boot was finally forced open and we set off by torchlight through the pine woods to our right.

It was 2.15am and there was not a chink of light through the trees as we made our way uphill, accompanied by the sound of our heavy breathing and the cracking of twigs and branches underfoot.

Ten minutes later, we emerged into a clearing and a strange, grey half-light that picked out the landscape but simultaneously left everything looking washed out. The day had not quite woken up yet. We decided to stay in what light there was by contouring round through long grass and boggy ground to follow the edge of the trees for about half a mile.

When the line of the forestry took a sharp right turn we went with it, heading steeply uphill on the well-worn staircase of muddy steps in the grass. The hard work had begun. The first part of climbing is always torture and, on a morning like this when the heat is so oppressive that you can't seem to catch a breath, it seems doubly so. There was also the small matter of the earlier car pushing to take into consideration.

We were in tee-shirts but already we were sweating buckets. The only option was to plod on, stopping every five minutes for a sip of water from our bottles. Conversation was kept to a minimum, a few caveman-like grunts and monosyllabic questions and answers the limit of the dialogue. You need to save your breath for breathing.

But then there was the sunrise and I spotted the summit cairn ahead on the skyline and the whole manner of the ascent changed. There was a spring in our step. It was as if we had wiped the slate clean and were just starting the walk. All the effort that had gone before to reach this point became irrelevant.

Suddenly the landscape opened up. We saw other mountains starting to peek up from every direction. I looked back and saw the height gained, felt the gentle, warm breeze taking away the dampness from my shirt. The grass and mud of the push upwards was left behind and we were on a path of a more comfortable gradient, something solid to plant our feet on which became almost like walking on the flat.

Mullach nan Coirean means 'the top of the corries' and there are five dropping down from the long, twisting spine of the mountain. The view west from the summit cairn leads the eye over the Firth of Lorn and the wild delights of distant Ardgour while, to the east, there is Stob Ban, which was our next target.

The ridge onwards winds its way through and over glowing, copper-coloured rocky stacks, like piles of pennies ready to topple over with one flick of the finger. The reddish hue of the mountain contrasts starkly with the white quartzite screes of Stob Ban dead ahead. From this point, with the pale rocks scattered over the vegetation of the slope, Stob Ban's profile is that of a sleeping woman's face, a grey veil draped over her features as she rests in stony silence.

The final push to the grey lady's forehead is on a loose path consisting of shattered white rock which crunches and tinkles underfoot, a stony carpet akin to broken glass and seashells. All the way up I couldn't help but glance to my left where there was a huge drop down into the corrie.

By the time we reached the summit of Stob Ban, a light mist had dropped on us and it took the temperature down with it. From tee-shirt walking at 3am, we were now in heavy jackets and fleeces at 6am. It was time for breakfast and a lie-down on the slabs which hold the pile of white rocks that mark the summit.

We were chuffed with our achievement so we decided to share our exhilaration by phoning Malcolm's wife Ellen. Unfortunately, folk who are fast asleep may not share your enthusiasm for the joys of the morning, so the call ended abruptly. Dawn is a wonderful thing only if you are awake.

The route down follows the rocky east ridge and we dropped quickly into the gorgeous greenery of the glen. By 8am we were at the car, so mellowed out that even the thought of the return road trip to Glasgow did not bother me. I could even handle the prospect of another car push. We were tired, filthy and had that faraway look you have only at moments of extreme fatigue and satisfaction.

As we were changing for the journey home, a taxi pulled up. A big guy in full hillwalking gear alighted, saw us and then sauntered over.

"You are going up the hill?" he asked in a foreign accent.

"No, we've just been up." He looked at us for a moment then slowly walked away. I suppose he thought we had escaped from somewhere secure. It was a look I was getting used to.

For Malcolm, the day had been a revelation. It was hard to equate this Malcolm with the one who had reacted so violently to the idea of early starts. For Fergus, however, the night patrol was just a non-starter.

When we first set out with the intention of doing the Munros, we had a blank canvas. Like most walkers with this ambition we started by doing the nearest hills to our base, so the likes of Ben Lomond, Ben Vorlich and Beinn Narnain were the first to fall.

Fergus and I had been operating under the eight-hour rule for our day jaunts. Even at that, our time frame was limited. A 7am start let us tackle most hills between Glasgow and Bridge of Orchy and to Killin in the other direction, but no further.

The problem was always going to be how to get those hills that were so tantalisingly close to the edges of our perimeter during a working day, but that challenge would be addressed later. There was plenty to be getting on with and jaunts up Beinn Chabhair, Ben Vane and Meall nan Tarmachan had doubled our tally.

At this point we were joined by Malcolm. The three of us had worked together in Aberdeen and Malcolm was keen to get out on the hills again after moving to Glasgow.

We would go out once a week, picking the hill and the day the week before, then heading out no matter what kind of weather was in store. With three of us, the driving was in rota and we started totting up the peaks. I was also managing to work my way into the Cairngorms and the Angus and Perthshire Munros on holidays and days off.

Forays up the Loch Lomond road were almost becoming routine. One driver and two weary passengers in the morning, a mountain or two and then a stop at the Drover's Inn at Inverarnan for a pint in front of a welcome fire on our way home.

The Drover's is one of these establishments that everyone should visit once in their life. The old coaching inn has the stuffed wildlife, kilted barmen and all the old – and I mean old – fixtures and fittings employed in a bid to play up to a romantic image of Scotland.

It is always funny to watch the shock on the faces of people who have never been there before. On occasion we have even seen a horse standing at the bar. Once we watched an American family trying to have lunch while the hoofed moocher was trying to grab food scraps from their plates.

The Drover's has a roaring fire and, on a freezing autumn or winter day, that is exactly what is needed. It is fair to say we sometimes did not feel like moving again when we were settled down in the heat. The minutes were counted out in the hope they would stretch beyond 60 seconds, anything to avoid having to go back to the daily grind.

Our confidence on the hills was growing. We were learning by our mistakes. Navigation was self-taught and we gobbled up every piece of advice we could find on routes.

Our gear was also improving. We had started our days in the outdoors wearing cotton polo shirts or tees, checked padded shirts from Millets that seemed more suited for building sites, and woollen crew neck jumpers. An old Army Surplus jacket completed the top half and it was Ron Hill joggers and sometimes denim shorts – yes, denim shorts – over that.

Ah, the Army Surplus store. Whatever happened to them? They were like the armed robber's convenience store, a place you could buy an old commando jacket, a black balaclava that covered your face and a handy-sized holdall that would take a selection of burglar's tools and even a sawn-off shotgun if required. Coincidentally, there always seemed to be an Army Surplus store near a bank. Perhaps that is why we don't see them any more – all the crooks are running the banks now. That and the fact the Army needs all its surplus in these days of cut, cut, cut.

High hair was also the fashion in these days, which added about two feet to your height. If you had seen us setting off for the hills in the early days, you could have been forgiven for thinking we were a downmarket Dexy's Midnight Runners tribute band wandering around looking for our tour bus.

We always had decent socks and boots, though, and the waterproofs, although they were not as sophisticated as today's models, did an adequate job. Gloves were hit and miss but the woolly hat was a belter. It was bright red and, when pulled down over your head and face leaving just a slot for the eyes, it made you look like a postbox. If you stood still for too long there was always the danger that some near-sighted old dear would try to shove her letters into that gap. It was also incredibly hot. No matter how cold it was outside, when you pulled that hat off it felt as if you had been in a steam bath.

With the overload of cotton, wool and denim, any consistent rainfall meant you returned to the car at the end of the day weighing twice as much as when you had started.

But the joggers and denims were replaced with knee-length breeches – homemade – then, later, the real McCoy, with heavier, warmer material, too warm, in fact, to be comfortable in hot weather. The woollen jumpers and big shirts were discarded in favour of fleeces but it would be a while before we moved away from the cotton tees and polo shirts.

Man-made fabrics were still a way off for us. We upgraded our rucksacks to the name of the moment, Berghaus, supremely tough and waterproof. The days of soggy sandwiches were over.

Even now, though, I refuse to spend a fortune on hill gear. What is the point of spending £400 on a jacket that is likely to get ripped when you're pulling yourself up over rocks?

One veteran mountain guide once told me that he regularly bought his gear from a well-known discount fashion store. His take was that you were paying silly money for the newest jackets which boasted extra zips – and a hike of £50 – from last year's model.

As he said: "Why would you need more zips in an outdoors jacket? The more zips you have, the more chance there is of water getting in."

As we nicked away here and there at the fringes of the Munro list, the elephant in the room was trumpeting louder and about to go on the rampage. It was time to broaden the horizons.

Starting ever earlier in the mornings was not a popular idea. Less sleep followed by longer car journeys and a more frantic rush to get back were not the solution. None of us were keen on that idea, Malcolm least of all.

Despite being a keen sailor and taking part in competitions which necessitated early starts, he was definitely not a morning person. When Fergus and I decided that we could set off at 6am one day to drive up to the Drumochter Pass and do the round of four Munros there, Malcolm was apoplectic.

"Six o'clock? In the morning? What time is that?"

So while Fergus and I chatted away on the drive up the A9,

Malcolm was slumped over in the back looking like he had the worst hangover in the world.

At least motoring up the A9 was a change for Fergus, taking him away from our more traditional journeys up the A82 and the constant reminder of the caramel slice. I don't think I have ever seen anyone more traumatised by a piece of home baking.

His agony had been going for almost a year, ever since we had descended from a walk to the car park underneath the power station at Inveruglas, just beyond Tarbet on the Loch Lomond road. We were always more than a little peckish at the end of a walk and, when Fergus spotted a burger van in the car park, he decided to treat himself.

Nice wee caramel slice, just the job. He came back to the car looking shell-shocked. I didn't get the chance to ask what was up.

"Do you know how much that cost me?" he asked. "90 pence. 90 pence for a caramel slice. That is twice the rate in Glasgow."

"Maybe that's why it's also known as millionaire's shortbread," I added helpfully, reflecting that only Fergus would know the market rate for a caramel slice.

"He'll certainly be a millionaire with prices like that."

All the way home in the car, the conversation returned to the great bakery rip-off, and it was brought up almost every time we sped past the car park on our way further north.

If it wasn't, neither Malcolm nor I were slow to bring up the subject.

"Want to stop for a caramel slice, Fergus?"

"Somebody should report that bastard. He's making fortunes by fleecing walkers. It's a disgrace."

It was like being in the presence of a Vietnam veteran having flashbacks. The horror, the horror.

3
Flip Flop

I'M ONE OF LIFE'S pessimists. I'm a glass half-empty type of guy, and a lot of the time that glass also has something unpleasant floating in it.

When it comes to world affairs, politics, work and personal and financial health, I always fear the worst. I also find it takes a great deal of effort to trust what anyone says. Cynical beyond belief. Maybe that's what a lifetime of working in newspapers does for you.

The legendary Skye mountain guide Gerry Ackroyd had a mantra: Trust everything – and trust nothing. He was referring particularly to the unpredictability of the terrain in the Black Cuillin but it also seems to capture perfectly the blurred lines between optimism and pessimism in the hills. In the great outdoors I emerge from a cocoon of pessimism transformed into a beautiful butterfly of optimism. There is never a bad day on the hills, some are just better than others. Rain, snow, high winds, blistering heat, there is always something good to be found. There has never been a day on the mountains when I have thought: "You know what? I'd rather be at work."

Hoping for the best while planning for the worst underpins my positive outlook. When things go wrong, I can tell myself that I knew there would be a setback and can adjust my plans accordingly.

I tend to look for the good news in the weather forecast, for instance. If the outlook is for rain sheeting down most of the day, I look for the little pocket where it will be dry and try to plan around that. If I stare out of the window and it is still raining, I reckon it will soon pass. If there is a lovely high pressure system nearby, I know that it will soon be over the area I am in. All nonsense, of course, but I like to keep the faith. I hate to concede that any chance to get out in the hills will be waylaid.

My climbing buddies used to shake their heads at such optimism. We would be sitting indoors, gazing out of the window at the rain bouncing so hard off the road that it appeared to be rebounding back into the sky. I would say: "Ach, it will be okay in a minute." It was the cue for sniggers all round.

I load the dice in my favour when I go out at night, picking times when the weather looks most settled. My strategy does not always work, but who wants to venture out when it's fair all the time? Brooding mist and cloud with dampness in the air can be far more atmospheric.

When I set off to do the three Munros on the Creag Meagaidh circuit I had been buoyed by the forecast the night before. Clear skies, good visibility and no wind, with just a hint of low cloud. But the word had not reached as far as Creag Meagaidh.

It was May 1 but the peaks were snow-capped and the ridges had the remains of some serious cornices. As I set off up the A9 after work, I began to doubt the weather forecast. The high point of the road, the Drumochter Pass, is often a good guide to what is round the corner. On this night, it was not looking good. The experience on Na Gruagaichean had made me wary of tackling the hills in poor visibility at these hours. I was not keen to relive that scenario.

When I arrived at the car park around 2.30am the weather had not improved, but I remained optimistic. The forecast for clear skies was out but hopefully just by a short time. I decided to rest in the belief that the better conditions would arrive.

Sleeping in a car is an art I have never really mastered. Often if I do manage to drop off for a bit, I wake up with my facial extremities freezing and with a sore throat. Then there are the aches and pains I associate with having been stuffed into a tight box. I am convinced that no sleep at all is better than a couple of hours followed by a rude and uncomfortable awakening.

By 4.30 I'd had enough. It was time to set off even though the weather had not lifted. It would soon – I was convinced. The chill was bitter and I needed to warm up.

Creag Meagaidh, 'the bogland rock', is a nature reserve, but nothing was stirring. Even the wildlife appeared to be reluctant to venture out as I headed up the superb path which winds its way into the massive bowl of Coire Ardair. The light was trying its best to break through but it was still dark enough to require a head torch.

I planned to do the three Munros on the circuit, so I was heading first for the south ridge of Carn Liath, 'the grey hill'. Grey was certainly the colour of the day.

The path through the trees is tight and the early stages saw me pelted with sopping wet branches and bushes which leave every square inch of your gear soaking. The temperature was low.

Then suddenly I was out of the trees on to more open ground and that is when the wind kicked in and made me shiver. When I hit the flat, stony summit of Carn Liath I was cold and wet but, with the cloud a thick blanket all around me, the wind had at least dropped.

Stob Poite Coire Ardair, 'the peak of the pot of the little corrie', is the next objective. The route onwards goes over a couple of minor Tops and the trek was undertaken in eerie stillness, with nothing to see except the blurred outline of the next rise on the stony ridge and the occasional rusted fence posts of a long-ruined barrier.

At this time of the morning when your body is already at a low, these conditions can turn what should be an exciting, beautiful ridge walk into a soul-destroying trudge. A few snow banks had to be turned along the way, adding to the frustration of getting to the summit.

The main cairn of Stob Poite Coire Ardair, normally a superb viewpoint, was just another pile of rocks in the mist. I have often thought that if you wanted to cheat your way round the Munros you could assemble various formations of rocks in your back garden, take a photograph and then claim you were on this hill or that hill. The proof of completing this Munro, therefore, was a snap I could have taken 3,000 feet lower down.

The day could only get better so I moved on, dropping into The Window, the prominent V-shaped gap in the ridge line between Stob Poite Coire Ardair and Creag Meagaidh. The cloud was starting to lift, giving me a glimpse of some of the delights about to unfold. The forecast weather had arrived, albeit four hours late.

Ach well, mighty Meagaidh and its spectacular scalloped corries would soon make up for the soulless trudge that had been the walk so far. But it was just at the very moment that my misplaced optimism was revealed to be a sham.

As I crossed the deep snow that filled The Window, I felt a freezing wetness in my right boot. No surprise, really, considering that the heel of my boot had come away from the main body, leaving it flapping around uselessly. I would have been as well wearing a flip flop – there was to be no Creag Meagaidh for me today. Even my less ambitious hope of having dried out before getting back to the car was now in tatters.

It was a long, slow, squelchy slog back down Coire Ardair, the beauty of its vegetation showing its finest colours in the emerging sunshine proving little consolation. A glance backwards towards the goliath rock walls of Meagaidh and the dark little lochan lying underneath them only served to increase the feeling of frustration and self-pity.

The sum total of a long drive, virtually no sleep and a cold, wet trudge was two Munros with no views and having to turn my back on possibly the only saving grace of the day.

My optimism had been shattered. Once again, I was starting to doubt the wisdom of night-time excursions.

It is hard to know where my enthusiasm for the mountains came from. It certainly was not hereditary. I do not have anyone from the family tree who strode around the Alps or the Himalayas in the great days of exploration. Considering my childhood experiences of the great outdoors, it is a wonder I did not remain locked in a darkened room for ever, terrified to go near anything resembling a hill.

My first foray was with the Boy Scouts during the mid-1960s in my hometown of Dundee. Those were the days when every young boy was press-ganged by his parents into joining either the Scouts or the Boys Brigade. There was no escape – you would think they wanted rid of you.

Life really is unfair when you are a child. My parents also insisted I went to Sunday school despite the fact they never ventured inside a church. When I asked why this was I was told: "Oh, you don't want to make the mistakes we did. This will make you a better person."

It did not. My two abiding memories of Sunday school are of annoyance and frustration at seeing all the bounty handed in for the harvest festival and the fact that I could not sample any of it despite feeling I was starving at the time; and putting my hand in a pile of puke on the pews that had been left by some other under-nourished kid forced to spend the morning in church.

The Scout troop I joined was on a downward spiral. They were based in an old part of Dundee where houses were being torn down and families moved out to housing schemes on the edge of the city. Numbers were dropping fast. Other Scout troops would go on week-long camps, but we did not have the numbers to justify such a venture. The solution was for us to join one of the bigger, better troops at their camp.

That explains why our small but perfectly formed team of six were sent off to Tarfside on the banks of the River Esk with a 40-strong contingent from another troop.

They were the real deal – all turned out in smart uniforms, every woggle in line, not a dib or a dob out of place. They looked like an army regiment dressed for a parade; we looked like the Taliban on Dressdown Friday.

But where the other Scout troop were spick and span, we were full of street smarts. Where they could make a fire by rubbing two sticks together, we could make a fire by rubbing two of the other Scouts together.

We had a guy called Whacko, a nickname he gained through having a preference for hurling a wooden mallet at anyone within distance. You soon learned the choreography of his movements and the gathering accumulation of his bad language to know exactly when to duck before the wooden missile whizzed by your head.

Our team of six won all the camp competitions, from football to frog spotting, athletics to bridge building. But the others did not seem to care. They wanted to be sporting and play the game – we wanted to win. It was almost as if they felt sorry for the street urchins from the bad side of town.

That attitude changed on the night we were awakened in our sleeping bags by a piercing scream after lights out. We all clambered out to see one of their senior troop members being helped out, blubbering, from his tent. The poor fellow had climbed into his sleeping bag for the night and, when his feet reached the bottom of the bag, he found a dead adder. Of course, he did not know the snake was dead when his feet brushed against it. His screams testified to that. No-one ever confessed to the crime – but the reptile had been whacked with a mallet.

My second – and final – outdoors experience as a Boy Scout was also an eye-opener. Four of us were taken to the youth hostel in Glen Doll on a snowy Friday night in December. But the adult leading the group left early on the Saturday morning because he was going on a night out with his wife. He told us he would come back to collect us on the Sunday.

Nowadays, he would probably be arrested for child neglect, but back then it didn't seem to matter if you abandoned a group of kids in the wilderness for a couple of days. After all, what could possibly go wrong? Four teenagers, left to amuse ourselves in wild, winter conditions…

Left to our own devices, we went for a walk on the Saturday, no compass, no map, no proper gear, into Corrie Fee. Glen Doll has seen its share of mountain tragedies – it is probably down to sheer luck there was not another one. We thought it was funny to fall into holes covered by deep snow. We arrived back in darkness, soaked, with no idea where we had been nor the possible danger we had been in.

That situation was not unusual back then. We were looking at Malcolm's old diaries one day and one of the entries mentioned that he had once been on the Aonach Eagach, the infamous ridge in Glen Coe, when he was just 13 years old as part of a Sunday school group. It read simply: "It was a bit scary." That's like saying Saddam Hussein was "a bit of a rascal".

It turned out that the adult in charge of the group was trying to work his way round the Munros, so he used the opportunity of having the Sunday school bus to visit far-flung hills he needed to climb.

You can just picture the newspaper headlines if he did that today: MOUNTAIN NUT TOOK YOUNG BOYS UP THE AONACH EAGACH.

Despite that inauspicious start, in the summer of 1992 I found myself sitting under the summit block of the Cobbler, having lunch in a sun trap while looking down over the still waters of Loch Long.

It was midweek, but the slopes and ridges of the three-pronged hill were crawling with people, like ants over a picnic.

The Cobbler, or Ben Arthur to give it its Sunday name, is not a Munro but it is one of the finest mountains in Scotland. From the humble intention of having a meal out in the sunshine instead of lazing in bed recovering from another stressful night in the office, far greater things were to come. A couple of friends working on a rival paper and on similar shifts decided this was a great idea and soon it was a regular outdoors party.

One day each week Fergus, Jim and myself explored the minor peaks of Lomondside, or headed into the Trossachs, or trekked into the Campsies. We were ramblers then and the only allowance towards specific hill gear was a good pair of boots and reliable waterproofs.

Some of the walks – Coilessan Glen, Ben A'an and the Ben Dubh horseshoe, for example – were as good as many of the bigger slopes we would come to scale regularly.

For someone finding their feet on the big hills again after so long, Ben Lomond was a natural progression, its motorway path, lined with basking adders in the lower reaches, proving a simple ascent.

Ben Vorlich was next, a long, grassy, sweaty push up from Coiregrogain on a sunny day. The mountain bug was starting to bite and the itch to get out more often was growing steadily. One-day walks were not enough – we needed more.

We decided to use a holiday week to walk the West Highland Way (WHW), but we would do it in four days not the usual five-to-seven most walkers take. This would be a bit more hardcore, 25 miles a day, and to make sure there was no temptation to duck out at any point for a day in any one of the many pubs straddling the route, we did it for charity. All along the 96 miles our eyes were gazing 3,000 feet upwards. That is where we really wanted to be.

We were dreaming of the big hills but, at that point, nothing more. The walks we were undertaking were within an hour's radius of Glasgow and would take only four or five hours at most.

There was no leeway in our current position. Pointing out yet another Munro from the WHW, Fergus rattled off the numbers and remarked that it would take a lifetime for us to complete them.

With a young family and a heavy workload, the chances of me

taking on a round of Munros seemed as likely at that moment as walking on the moon.

The blisters had hardly cleared from our expedition when Fergus and I were off up Beinn Narnain. We took the route over A'Chrois, the Cross, a satellite peak of the Munro, and headed over the rocky ridge to the trig point at the summit, then returned over the back and round the path with The Cobbler on the right to reach the car at the foot of Loch Long.

Three down, now I just needed to find a way to get up the other 274 on the list (there were 277 Munros then, the total increased to 284 in 1997).

All this time, I was being egged on by some of the older guys in my office with a previous hill life. One or two were serious mountain men, although age and work commitments had scaled back their outings, and they were forever pushing me towards bigger and better things. To hear their tales of far-off peaks and life-affirming, sometimes life-threatening, days out filled me with excitement.

Those inspirational words, coupled with the brand-new Scottish Mountaineering Club (SMC) Munros book I had received as a Christmas present from Alison (mainly, I think, so I could look at the pretty pictures – nothing as daft as trying to scale any of them) merely helped to confirm that this was my future.

The SMC book was our bible. All these beautiful places and exotic-sounding mountains in parts of Scotland I had never even heard of, let alone visited. Glen Coe was a mystery, a place where only real mountaineers would dare to tread, and we were a long way from that.

I knew my way round the Perthshire and Angus countryside when I was a child, mainly due to being forced into my dad's car at weekends at a metaphorical gunpoint.

Having a car then was a novelty for many and we had to drive hundreds of miles on a Sunday just to show that we appreciated it. A two or three-hour car journey driving around winding country roads only to stop at a field somewhere, take an hour or so to lay out the picnic, eat it in two minutes flat and then reverse the whole process to get home before dark. It is hard to see how that was enjoyable for my mum and dad; three hacked-off kids moaning in the car with the occasional bout of vomiting thrown in, but they persevered.

To my shame, I was largely ignorant of my own country. Not that I was alone. For a fiercely patriotic nation, it never ceases to amaze me how many Scots have never been north of Perth. They are as tribal as any ancient clan. The two people I have met with the greatest knowledge of Scotland have been an Englishman and a Dutchman.

A flick through the Munro book would continually reinforce my ignorance but also my sense of wonder, a constant reminder that I wanted to visit every one of those peaks. I wanted to become an explorer in my own country, a Magellan of the Munros.

Anywhere north of the Great Glen was unexplored territory: Fisherfield, Torridon, Knoydart, Arkaig, they were areas of dark, brooding mountains that could just as well have been on the other side of the world, so removed were they from my comfort zone.

The great, twisting ridges of Glen Shiel and Glen Affric, with their massed peaks of tongue-twisting Gaelic names, their sinister translations sounding like a warning: you can look, but you can't touch.

Mountains classified by group names such as the Strathfarrars, the Mullardochs, the Fannichs, chains of individually chiselled shapes that acted like siren songs to awestruck recruits such as I.

Altnaharra, Coulags, Oykel, Kinlochewe, habitations that sound like they could have been invented by Tolkien but, instead, were gateways to so much adventure.

One picture that resonated particularly was that of Maol Chean-dearg in Glen Carron. Its name translates as 'bare, red-headed hill', but its profile in the book was of a menacing, black, bare sheet of rock, soaring into the clouds with streaks of snow and ice striping its sides like a massive granite tiger, ready to claw and bite the head off anyone foolish enough to attempt to climb it. The paths were ice-covered, the sky was dark and full of the threat of snow and there was a walker striding ominously into its maw wearing a woollen sweater and a flat cap.

It was a revelation. I had assumed that these terrifying-looking hills would be the domain only of people dressed for an expedition to Everest, but here was an ordinary person – well-equipped, no doubt, and with a great knowledge and experience of what he was doing – nonchalantly about to climb this beast.

That was the moment I knew that I could do all the Munros. If a guy in a woolly jumper and a bunnet could conquer this hill, then there was nothing to stop me.

4
The Deer Grand National

IT'S A LONG RUN just to get to the foot of Gleouraich and Spidean Mialach, especially after a hard day and night in the office. But I had my intrepid explorer's hat on so off I went on the four-hour run to paradise.

The heat during the previous day had been stifling, and thick mist gripped the floor of the glen during the latter part of the journey. Spidean Mialach means 'hill of the louse', not a particularly appealing name. It is more likely to refer to midges, also an unwelcome prospect, but the air was happily and rather unexpectedly midge free.

The hills are on the Quoich estate, where stalking is big business. The main advantage for the walker, however, is that the paths giving access to, and across, the hills are superb. The circuit starts on a well-cut path which pushes up through thick stands of pink rhododendron before opening out, and I was making swift progress up the hillside despite not being able to see three feet in front of me.

By the time I was about 500ft up from the road, I could see a faint, red glow appearing through the mist. It became stronger with every step I took until virtually the whole hillside was cloaked with a reddish tinge. Then I popped up through the low-lying band of cloud into total visibility.

It was a classic inversion – everything below me was invisible, shrouded in a sea of white cotton wool, while above, sweeping across the slopes of the hill, were the ochre streaks of a 4am sunrise.

Many hill-goers can live their entire life without experiencing an inversion. When they do, it is the stuff of wonder. When you set out in the early hours they become 10 a penny, yet every time they instil a sense of wonder. This was one of the most intense I had ever seen. My head and shoulders were clear but the lower half of my body was still almost hidden, creating an almost cartoon-like quality.

I kept heading up, always finding the path of least resistance. But the inversion was not finished yet. As I rose, so did this phenomenon, always staying just a few feet behind me, as if not sure of the route.

As the path swung out to traverse along the side of a grassy face on the south-west ridge, I looked down to my left to try to catch a glimpse of the little finger of Loch Quoich which splits the flow of the mountain from Sgurr a'Mhaoraich over the divide, but it was hidden under a sea of cloud. My route then shifted round to the right for the final push.

By the time I was sitting at the summit of Gleouraich, the cloud base was a vast, white ocean, covering everything in Scotland except the high peaks, which jutted out like islands from the sea. I felt as if I was the only man on earth.

Gleouraich translates as 'the peak of uproar' or 'noise', a reference to the bellowing of the stags when in rut, but today there was hardly a sound. It was as though the weather was holding its breath. I stood at the huge, beautifully engineered beehive cairn and absorbed my surroundings. It was one of those all-too-rare moments of serenity, a time to drink in the majesty of the occasion for as long as possible.

The heat was stifling, so the inversion was going nowhere fast. The grand highway eastwards from the summit of Gleouraich provided new views down into the remote northern corries with the peaks of the South Shiel Munros popping up above the cloud sheet behind, seven in a row. As I walked along towards Spidean the inversion sat just below the ridge.

As I approached the drop into the low point between my two hills, I could not see any ground. The pass, the Fiar Bhealaich, had vanished. The cloud was pouring over the col like a massive waterfall and Spidean appeared as an island I could not reach.

Logic told me the path went into the mist and continued easily up the next slope, but my sleep-deprived brain was once again questioning my reasoning. What if there was just a bottomless pit once I stepped into that cloud?

It sounds mad now but that little doubt was nagging away, providing a mental obstacle to overcome. After a few minutes' debate with myself, I continued tentatively, descending into the cloud to find – surprise, surprise – terra firma and no problems.

If I had thought normality had been restored, the Quoich hills had one last surprise. As I took a diagonal line down the open hillside, the band of cloud was still clinging on as far as the eye could see. And heading towards me, but still hundreds of feet below, was a figure.

This was a first. Never before had I seen anyone on the hills at this time of the morning, but here he was striding uphill on the same trajectory as I was going down. What kind of lunatic would be climbing a mountain at this time of the morning?

I stopped – and so did he.

I stood still – so did he.

I waved – so did he.

I dropped my rucksack to the ground to get a drink. So did he. Only now he had a little rainbow encircling his head. Something was not right. As we drew closer and closer, he started to fade away until, when I was just a matter of feet away from meeting this kindred spirit, he vanished.

Then it hit me – the person I had alighted on heading up the hill was me.

It was a Brocken Spectre, a light reflection of yourself often seen during inversions. With the cloud below me and the brilliant sunshine behind, I was reflected into the cloud and then bounced back as a mirror image of myself.

I had seen a Brocken Spectre on a few occasions. The name comes from the Brocken peak in Germany, which is said to provide the ideal conditions to conjure up this striking illusion. The strange event was first recorded back in the 1800s and there are tales of walkers being so spooked by the sudden appearance of these shadowy giants they almost fell to their deaths in panic. Normally, they are huge figures, standing stock still, with a large round head similar to an Afro hairdo and the legs tapering ever outwards near the bottom, as if the figure is wearing flares. The spookiest thing about it is the 1970s style.

This one was different. It appeared to be just the same height as myself and was walking freely. The photograph I managed to take does not do the incident justice – it looks like an alien in a ball of light.

When my colleagues at work asked what I had been up to that morning I told them: "I was on a mountainside 150 miles away at 6am playing with myself."

Probably similar to what some of them had been doing at home.

The heatwave during the summer of 1995 seemed to go on forever and it probably sealed my love affair with night-time walking. I had endured my couple of bad days early in the adventure and had not given up. Now, with the weather playing fair, never again would I doubt the wisdom of what I was doing.

Walking into the sunrise can lift even the dullest hills. The Monadhliath hills, for instance, are not the most highly-rated among walkers, which is understandable. They are not soaring, jagged peaks providing hands-on clambering. They do not make the heart race faster. But on a stunning day, as I drove up the A9 towards the starting point at the back of Newtonmore, I knew the circuit of three – Carn Dearg, Carn Sgulain and A'Chailleach – was destined to be a grand expedition.

No thoughts of a kip in the car, it was almost light already despite the fact it was only 2.15am. Why waste a second of good weather? No head torch needed, my night vision was good enough and the track was lit by the rising sun.

A short walk along a level pathway, then just before the house at Glenballach the route turned north through the fields and up a stony track through the steep-sided glen by the gently flowing Allt Fionndraigh. This was no-brain walking, just putting one foot in front of the other while taking in the sound of silence, the beautiful reds, greens and yellows of the terrain and the rapidly unfolding vistas of Gleann Ballach.

Carn Dearg is 'the red hill', but it was hard to see how its name was justified today, green being the predominant colour. When I hit the summit of Carn Dearg the vagaries of morning light became clear to me. Although I had been walking along convinced it was full daylight, the view – and the pictures I took – showed that Carn Sgulain and A'Chailleach were just black outlines in the distance with a yellow-tinged sky lit up behind them. The route onwards is little more than a stroll in good weather – in poor conditions it could pose problems with navigation – a gently rolling walk over short, clipped grass with a mostly well-worn path to follow.

It seems I hardly conceded or gained any height at all from Carn Dearg by the time I hit the summit of Carn Sgulain. It is a fairly featureless lump, and again it is hard to see how it justifies its name, 'the hill of the basket', as it is hard to discern any real definable shape.

A downhill run over soggy moss and grass into a deep V and then a short push up similar terrain took me to the final summit, A'Chailleach. It is a far more shapely affair, especially when viewed from the east where its scooped corrie is prominent. The name means 'the old woman', after the Cailleach Bheur who wandered these hills, her siren voice calling deer hinds in for milking. A swift run down from A'Chailleach picks up the track alongside the Allt a'Chaorainn and I arrived back at the car with a smug feeling of self-satisfaction.

Even though it had been an easy day in good conditions, I was sweating and my trousers were mud-spattered. I looked like a man who has been in the wilderness for seven hours. That obviously puzzled the gentleman who had pulled up in his car, ready to set off on the same walk.

I said hello and sat down to take off my boots. He looked at me quizzically then, probably finding my appearance hard to take in, said: "Have you just been up the hill?"

I wanted to say: "No. I just walked up that track a little way, popped behind a bush and then rolled around in mud and shit to give the impression I have been."

Has no-one ever seen a man climbing mountains in the middle of the night before?

I was on a roll now and, exactly a week later, I was heading up the A82 en route to Spean Bridge. My target this time was the twins of Stob Coire Sgriodain and Chno Dearg, which are situated at the hamlet of Fersit at the head of Loch Treig, the site of my first night walk.

Once again it meant driving past the old Hess house at Inverlair, but with a surety of knowing how the road progressed I was able to take the bends like a rally driver – a Nuremberg rally driver, obviously – as I headed to my starting point.

I set off walking at 2.30am with a gossamer mist steaming off the surrounding fields. It was almost cheating to call this night-time. The light was rising, and the heat was already beginning to bring out the sweat of the climb upward. The sky was filled with multi-coloured pastel streaks, as if an ethereal Degas had gone crazy with his brushes.

Sgriodain is 'the peak of the scree corrie' and after a walk through a field of cows and up grassy steps beside a small, tumbling stream, the mountain starts to show its character. I weaved in and out of little boulder groups, ever upward, and then over steeper, stonier ground with the majestic Loch Treig starting to hove into view far below.

The final push to the cairn is out on the flank, a panorama which takes the pain out of any ascent. Two hours after leaving the car, I was at the summit of Sgriodain. It is a magnificent perch, the perfect breakfast spot and, as I looked down, the West Highland railway line seemed like a Hornby miniature and Loch Treig was bathed in a fiery orange glow. It was the colour of Hell but showing the beauty of Heaven.

Chno Dearg is 'the red nut', most likely a name referring to the heather-clad slopes sweeping down to the north. The mountain is not that exciting but the view down to the dark lochan in the corrie is always a joy, and the run down the mountainside is easy. The midges were starting to stir, rising from the heather in clouds as I crashed my way down, but I was back at the car before 7am, too early for anything else but the birds and the cows to be stirring.

Maybe this was why it was the perfect spot to keep Hess. Cows. Our German friends are not fond of them. Sometimes they are downright terrified of them. It is one of these nuggets of valuable information you pick up while wandering the hills. This one came from a grizzled, wee Glaswegian called Wullie, a man from the Basil Fawlty camp of Anglo-German relations.

We met Wullie on a trek into the Ben Lui hills. He had a lived-in face, one that was currently occupied by lots of children if his cheeky enthusiasm was anything to go by. He could have been any age from 40 to 90. He had arms like Popeye – his lower arm muscles were wider than his waist – and he looked like he had been a superb climber. He seemed to have the strength of a bull and the grace of a ballet dancer. I had the feeling that if he fell down a mountain he would just bounce until he reached the bottom and then pick himself up, dust himself down and set off again without a care.

The best climbers always make it look so easy. Once I was on Tryfan in north Wales, a superb scrambler's peak, a 3,000-foot vertical, hands-on climb from the road right to the summit. As myself and a friend made our way up, we were comfortably passed by a group of six women. They were members of the Scottish Ladies' Climbing Club. Every one of them was slight and delicate, and they moved up the rock with consummate ease at incredible speed. It was like watching a line of black spiders racing up a grey wall.

Wullie certainly looked like he had been a spider in his day and he was good company as he walked along the track from Dalrigh, just up from Crianlarich. We were heading to the two Munros, Beinn Dubhchraig and Ben Oss, and he was going up one of his favourites, Ben Lui.

He was regaling us with a tale of a Second World War plane crash on that mountain and he was hoping to see some of the wreckage today. Maybe he was also intent on carrying all of it back down. He certainly looked fit enough.

Blocking the track a little further on was a herd of Highland cattle, lined up as if they were posing for a photoshoot for a McCowan's toffee wrapper. As we approached them, about 500 yards off to the right we could see a young couple struggling through a boggy field. They had obviously decided to give the coos a body swerve and were now toiling in the water-heavy pasture.

Wullie turned to us and said: "Hah, look at them. Germans."

"How do you know that? Did you speak to them earlier?"

"No, I just know they're German."

"Okay, how do you know that?"

"Easy. Everybody knows that Germans are terrified of cows."

"What, every German?"

"Aye. Mark my words, every time they see a cow they're off."

If it was that easy to scare the Germans then surely the Allies could have ended the Second World War earlier by parachuting a herd of heifers on to the front line.

We went our separate ways and thought nothing more of Wullie's comments until later when we crossed paths with the young couple from the bog. We quickly discovered they were German, and were also very nervous around the cows.

Now if this had been an isolated incident, I would have forgotten all about it. But it has happened time and time again. On a march out from Beinn Bhuidhe up at Loch Fyne, for instance, a group of us came across a family standing in front of a bovine roadblock, a herd of cows who had no intention of moving from the tarred road. One of our party, a no-nonsense country girl, just walked past the family and slapped one of the cows on the arse, immediately creating a clearway through the beasts. The family followed us through. They were German.

Malcolm had obviously enjoyed his previous nocturnal outing so much that he was back for more. We decided on Beinn Sgulaird, the lone hill which rises at the head of Loch Creran. He had sold the Ride of Frankenstein so, hopefully, this journey would not involve any pre-ascent car pushing. In fact, it was all rather pedestrian and dull, and we arrived at the car park in the forest at Elleric in reasonable fettle.

Well, apart from the fact that I missed the turn-off and then had to make a sharp manoeuvre to make the car park. The car did not like it one bit.

"That didn't sound too good," I said.

"Maybe because you tried to put it into reverse at 60 miles an hour," Malcolm said.

"I can't believe you are slagging my car. You're the man who bought a £50 car from Cochise or Geronimo or whatever his name was."

"I'm not slagging your car, just your reversing procedure."

Reversing procedure? Jeez, I was in the car with a would-be driving instructor.

It was breaking dawn as we set off on the track up Glen Ure, and it was there that we saw the Deer Grand National. It was one of those sights that could be seen only at that time of day.

As we approached a walled field on the right-hand side of the road, we noticed about 200 deer. They had obviously come down during the hours of darkness to feed while no-one was around. They had not reckoned on two lunatics wanting to climb a mountain at 4am.

At first they appeared to take no notice of us. Then one head jerked up quickly. Then another, and another. Now they were all on alert and we were the centre of attention. We stood still but they were starting to get nervous. A few barks of warning, a closing of the ranks. Then they began milling around, slowly, going in circles, weighing up their options, sticking together, none of them wanting to be left behind. They wanted to make a break for it but so far they did not appear to have decided which way was best.

We stayed stock still, sure that something was about to happen. Then one broke the spell and raced for the wall in front of us, clearing it with an effortless leap. Another one was close on its heels, then they were charging en masse like they were heading for Becher's Brook. The noise of their hooves broke like thunder in the damp stillness of the morning. We were watching a continuous brown streak moving at speed over the wall, across the road and off over the open ground to our left, almost impossible to define one animal from the other.

Suddenly it was all over and we were again surrounded by silence. It seemed incredible that only 30 seconds earlier we had just watched about 200 deer behave as if they were at Aintree.

Sgulaird's name, 'the hill of the hat', comes from its shape. From side on it could be argued that it looks like a large hat, bashed in at the top. Being a stand-alone Munro, the views from the large summit cairn are expansive, looking seaward over the Firth of Lorn towards Mull, although even that would struggle to top the Deer Grand National.

Sgulaird was also the peak that Malcolm's famous phrase "a bit iffy" came into use time and time again. I had learned long ago that if Malcolm uttered those words, it usually meant something approaching certain death was ahead.

So when he went forward to scout out the route and I heard:

"I wouldn't come up this way, it's a bit iffy", I decided to go another way. Malcolm, meanwhile, overcame his bout of iffiness to continue to the summit. It was two very tired and rosy-cheeked laddies who posed for pictures at the top with Loch Creran as a sparkling backdrop.

The warm, settled spell just went on and on and, after a baking hot day on Beinn Mheadhoin in the Cairngorms, it was back to the overnight assault on the Munros. But by my next foray into darkness the weather had started to become more unpredictable, and so as I drove up after work my hope of a fine day on the two outliers of Meall Greigh and Meall Garbh in the Ben Lawers range was looking extremely optimistic.

Nevertheless, I set off on the track past Machuim Farm with head torch lit but the mist and cloud must have been ticking off the same Munros because they stuck with me all the way on the slog to the summit. Unknown to me, a sheepdog had also been silently following my trail. I knew I should not have had the lamb in the canteen the night before.

As I left the summit cairn, the dog came barrelling out of the mist barking and snarling and tried to take a lump out of my leg. I instinctively dodged the snapping jaws and took a swing at it with my right boot. Again, no contact, but it then turned tail and disappeared back into the mist. I never saw it again.

The excitement over, I headed off on the long and bog-strewn ridge to Meall Garbh, still surrounded by thick cloud and that very fine smirr you seem to experience only in Scotland. Sightseeing was definitely not an option – that is, until I was about 10 feet from the summit. There I once again burst through the cloud to walk above another inversion.

This one was not so spectacular as Quoich, and only the very highest peaks were clear but I had an attic space of about six feet in which to sit and have breakfast in the sunshine while below the rest of the country shivered and became wet. It took a lot to prise me away knowing that in two minutes I would be back in the gloom.

I had not realised how long I had sat up there. When I came into work later that day, I was asked how I had managed to obtain a suntan from a night's sleep and a rotten, overcast day.

One week later and I headed north in the night. The head torch was on again as I went up from Mamore Lodge to scale Binnein Beag and Binnein Mor. Binnein Mor is a massive, tent-like peak which towers over its wee brother, a beautiful little pyramid sitting to the north in the protection of its bigger sibling. I made good progress up the track from Kinlochleven. By the time it was starting to get light I was on the lower slopes of Beag and it was clear going all the way on the snaking path through the jumble of boulders to the summit.

Unfortunately its bigger brother across the col was in a blacker mood and, after a long haul through the grey that shrouded the higher slopes, I was at the tumbled-down cairn on the short, level summit ridge. I sat for about 20 minutes in a rather optimistic show of defiance but the mist did not relent and I never saw a thing. It is one of the peaks that has denied me a view. I am beginning to think it is personal.

Finally, while the country was locked in a dry but bitterly cold snap that seemed to have lasted for weeks, Fergus and I headed into Glen Etive to climb Stob Coire'an Albannaich and Meall nan Eun. The temperature in Glasgow that day was -22, and on the track it felt like you were inhaling ice crystals. However the higher we climbed, the higher the temperatures rose. By the time we were on the summit we reckoned it was only about -16.

The final twist was that when the thaw finally arrived a week later I was witness to another, less welcome inversion – in my flat. The ceilings had descended to the floor as the frozen pipes in the loft expanded. But at least I could see the stars through the roof.

5
Creatures of the Night

THE DEVASTATION CAUSED to my flat kept me busy for a few months and the Munros, for once, had to take a back seat. It was not until late April that I was able to tick off Munro No.144.

Now I was poised to return to business seriously – and this time I would have company. One of my colleagues was curious about the mountain trips and mentioned that he would be keen to give it a try. Robert had not been out on the hills for 20 years but he had previously undertaken serious climbs and he was still fit.

When I explained that most of my walking was now undertaken at night, he expressed surprise but appeared to take the news in his stride. His only proviso for accompanying me was that he would have to be off work the next day. He could not imagine going straight back into the office after such an undertaking. Weakling.

So, on a beautiful morning in early May, he joined me as I headed for Glen Shiel straight after work. We were going to Lundie, just short of the Cluanie Inn, where a track gains access to a natural grouping of three Munros, Carn Ghlusaid, Sgurr nan Conbhairean and Sail Chaorainn.

It may seem brave to tackle three big hills for a first outing, but I had every faith in Robert. By this time my body was accustomed to travelling long distances and then walking in the mountains for hours while everyone else was tucked away for the night. But this was new territory for Robert. He was soon feeling the effects of travel sickness and, after a couple of hours, we had to pull over to the side of the road, where he threw up.

There was no question, however, of him pulling out at this stage. Anyway, I think he realised it would be a long walk back from Fort William if he chose to drop out. What, did you think I was going back? No chance.

When we reached our destination, it was starting to get light. I gave Robert five minutes to take in the beauty of the sunrise and then we prepared for action. And that was my first big surprise.

Robert wore a heavy woollen jersey and a flat cap, items that caught my eye.

Wait a minute – surely this wasn't the guy from the Munro book picture of Maol Chean-dearg, my early inspiration? No, it was not. It just seems that everyone back then wore this gear, as if they were expecting to pick up a bit of roofing work while up the hill.

I then asked gingerly about his waterproofs. He had a decent jacket, but then he pulled out what appeared to be a pair of red rubber trousers. I stared in astonishment.

"What the hell are they?"

"Waterproofs."

"Are they rubber?"

"No, they're golf waterproofs."

It's 2.30 in the morning and I am about to climb a hill with a man in a flat cap and red rubber trousers. He looked like a Hebridean heading for a fetish club.

They also looked like they weighed more than my entire rucksack and its contents. Luckily, it was not raining.

It took a bit of prodding to get Robert going. He seemed transfixed by the emerging beams of sunshine bringing the whole glen alive. The mountains seemed to be without end. On the south side of the road, the peaks of the nine-mile long South Shiel regiment were lined up for morning reveille with everything beyond, which had remained as shapes in the darkness on our drive up, showing as blue spectral lumps. Further down on the north of the A87, the North Shiel heights stole a march on the regal Five Sisters and, beyond that, jagged lines of The Saddle were flexing their muscles after a night's rest.

We started off on the old track heading west, but soon cut off to head north on an ever-improving path over grass and ground still soaking in morning moisture. After a bit of twisting and turning, the path takes a steeper trajectory, slicing back and forth across the south face of our first hill. A light wind caressed us as we turned right from the top of the path to emerge on more open ground, which leads without much effort to the summit cairn. This sits on the crumbling edge of the northern corrie, Corrie Sgreumh, 'the corrie of gloom', the view downwards one of steep rock and moss-covered craggy faces.

Carn Ghlusaid is 'the hill of movement', most probably referring to the sheets of unstable screes which roll down the northern wall, but the only movement was Robert's tongue. The second Munro, Sgurr nan Conbhairean, soared skywards, a heavenly-bound pyramid, the slopes showing no sign of having an end. Robert had done well for his first night mountain but now the real work was about to begin, and he knew it. He could not stop saying how far away and much higher Conbhairean was from here.

'The hill of the dog men' is a massive mountain and did look a long way off but the foreshortening, as always, was deceptive and about an hour later we were at the big pile of rocks after a steady push up the shattered, rocky terrain at what seemed to be a constant 90-degree angle. If you close your eyes it would be easy to picture hunters spying out the lands below before unleashing their hounds on the deer feeding far below.

The early sunlight we had experienced at ground level had not made it this far yet and, with remnants of snow still on the summit, it was chilly. So the red rubber pants came out. There was a picture taken for posterity and I am willing to listen to offers. I already have a bid of 400 Euros from Rob in Bishopbriggs.

Sail Chaorainn, 'the heel of the rowan trees', is only 30 minutes away. A big loss of height on a winding path through broken rock takes you to greener, softer ground and then gently upwards to the long, level summit ridge. There are three tops, the first of which is the highest despite your eyes trying to convince you otherwise. The lowest top, Tigh Mor na Seilge, looks the most impressive from here, a rocky, undulating wall which stretches off to the bounds of Glen Affric. To complicate matters further, this was the name applied to the highest peak in days gone by, another reference to hunting, which seems more apt than the modern one. Hidden away down to the right is one of the many caves in which Bonnie Prince Charlie is supposed to have taken refuge.

What goes up must go down but, in this case, it has to go up again to find the way back to the starting point. The prospect of re-ascending the heights of Conbhairean must be torture for many, but there is a bypass path which cuts out a lot of the re-climbing, leading instead to a long grassy ridge which heads south in easy stages. It terminates on the old military road which provides a direct route back to the car.

Robert was weary on this last stretch but he could not shake off the sheer beauty of being out on the hills at this time of day. I knew he would be back.

The next two outings were like night and day. Or day and night, to be precise. First, another Cairngorms day saw Beinn Bhreac and Beinn a'Chaorainn conquered before it was off on the relatively short drive through Arrochar to the head of Loch Fyne for the climb up to Beinn Bhuidhe.

The first hour-and-a-half are on a good track so, setting off at

2am was no sweat. It was almost a comparable feat to that of the remarkable Goran Kropp who, a few hours earlier, had reached the summit of Everest solo, without Sherpa help or oxygen. And he had cycled all the way from Sweden six months earlier. He really knew how to have a good time. It was like we were blood brothers.

Most of the time I try not to use a torch when walking in the dark. Usually, after about 10 minutes in the darkness, your vision has adjusted to the lack of light and unless it is pitch-dark you can make out where you are going. Artificial light often just means you take longer to adjust your vision.

It was still dark by the time I reached the start of the ascent path which rises steeply up the side of a tree-lined gully, but my night vision was working perfectly. The only sounds came from the rushing of the stream in the gorge and the occasional cry from the sheep on the other side, having been disturbed by my unexpected arrival.

About halfway up the first stage, there is a tricky section of rock above the drop that needs some handwork but, apart from the realisation that a fall here would be serious, there is no real difficulty. The thoughts that race through your mind at times like this make it seem far more of an issue than it is. Once past this minor moment of excitement, the hardest part is keeping track of the path which often seems to merge into the grassy terrain of various shades of yellow and orange which give the mountain its name.

I lost the path in the morning gloom and low cloud but kept my line to the next rise, where I could see the final wall of my objective looming ahead over a flat, wet floor. No problem if you are a heron but, for me, it would require delicate footwork to slither and slide through the boggy ground and small pools of water that dotted the landscape.

Being slightly off course presented me with another challenge. From the angle I had approached the wall, I could not see the main chink in the armour that would take me to the summit ridge. Normally you would climb this gully and then hang a left along the ridge on a solid path to the tumbled down trig point and summit cairn. But my compass was showing the summit dead ahead, so I reckoned I could ascend at any point along this line.

I chose one of the slits in the rock face, just about the width for two bodies side by side, and started heading up. This was fine at the start but, as I hauled my way up the increasingly greasy and tightening chimney, it was proving harder and harder to get a confident grip on anything.

Some of my holds were reduced to tugging on grass sticking out of the rock, my feet were slipping on the thick, cloying mud and there was a constant stream of water seeping down the black rock and under the wrist bands of my jacket. It was becoming harder with every pull-up.

I had to hope the conditions would ease or I would have to climb down and start again. That would not be ideal. It would be a nightmare trying to get down this loose, steep channel and a slip at any point, while probably not a killer, would be enough to inflict serious damage. I was also off the main drag so if I did fall or was injured, it would be sheer luck if anyone was to stumble across me soon. The sweat was pouring off me despite the chill. It was either the effort or the anxiety.

Then, just as if it seemed as if I was running out of options and holds, one final pull took me clear. The angle eased, the rock became more stepped and the route to the ridge was freed up.

I found the path, but something told me I was too far along the ridge. A swift check to the right showed that the top was just ahead. My reward for this gruelling and goosebump-inducing climb? No view and a blast from a vicious wind.

Another couple of hours and it would have been fine but often, at that time of the morning, the cloud is reluctant to clear the summits. Or maybe it's just Beinn Bhuidhe – I have not had a view in three attempts.

It is a steep run down but at least this time I found the right gully to descend. Just as I crested one grassy rise, I disturbed what looked like a large, brown dog tearing across the pasture. I have been told it was probably a hill fox. It certainly looked more than a match for any of the more common red variety. Maybe my arrival at that moment had ruined its plans for breakfast as it took off pronto and disappeared before I could take a picture.

A couple of weeks later Fergus and I were heading north for a weekend to rack up some serious numbers. The first day we drove to Lael, south of Ullapool, to do the four Beinn Dearg Munros. We did them clockwise starting on Eididh nan Clach Geala, then on to Meall nan Ceapraichean and Cona' Mheall and finally up to Beinn Dearg.

The col between Cona' Mheall and Beinn Dearg stares down into Coire Ghranda, 'the ugly corrie'. No place could be less aptly named. It is a beautiful spot. From our vantage point on the massive drystane dyke which divides this land, we saw a small plane which appeared to be in trouble. It sounded as if the engine had cut out and it was heading alarmingly close to the massive wall of Beinn Dearg. When it turned on its side and its wheels were almost running along the cliff face we felt sure that we were going to witness a disaster. But then the engine caught, the plane righted itself and soared upward to safety. A wave of the wings suggested that the pilot had been showing off for the tourists in the corrie.

The massive Dearg dyke never fails to amaze. It is the most consistently high man-made mountain wall of all – in places up to six feet – and it runs all the way down the north-west ridge. We followed it to its end then dropped off to cross the River Lael and then back to the car.

We stopped in Beauly for the night – no-one can accuse of us of not knowing how to have a good time – and then next morning headed for Glen Strathfarrar to do the circuit of four Munros there.

Strathfarrar, in my opinion, is the most beautiful glen in Scotland, but access is restricted, and only a restricted number of cars – usually about 20 – are allowed in at any one time. It always pays to get there by 9am. Any earlier and you are sent to the back of the queue by the gatekeeper; any later and you may see the sign: Glen Full. Honestly. It is such a bizarre sight to see cars waiting patiently in a line by this sign for someone to leave so they can take their place.

There is also the regular sight of car owners bartering with each other at the gate to pool vehicles and save a walk back along the road at the end of the day.

Fergus and I had just the one car but we managed to secure a lift back along the road from someone with more foresight.

It was time to get Robert back out among the creatures of the night, so the next outing was to Glenfinnan on the Mallaig road, deep in Jacobite country, for the Corryhully Horseshoe, two peaks which form a good natural circuit.

The first hour or so is on a good track and the weather forecast was fine, so we were happy to walk it in the dark. But when we arrived at the car park at 2.30am, the rain was thundering down and so we decided to wait it out. Fifteen minutes later and we were off under the famous railway viaduct, with first light still a bit off.

The wind was coming from the north and we were heading in from the south so the huge stag chomping happily on bushes at the side of the track never smelled us or heard us coming. We also had not seen this magnificent beast until the last second. I don't who panicked first, Robert or the stag, but the result was a crashing of bushes and a lot of anxiety. There is nothing like a huge, startled animal charging about to waken you up. The stag was a bit perturbed, too.

Just 10 minutes further up the track after the crossing of a stream, is situated the Corryhully Bothy, one of the better shelters. It even boasts electric lighting. Off to the right is the wonderfully named Streap, which means simply, 'climbing', the most impressive of a superb collection of peaks. The route between Streap and Sgurr Thuilm is one of the finest high passes in the country, eventually leading down into Glen Pean and through the Arkaig hills into Knoydart.

Sgurr Thuilm may be 'the peak of the rounded hillock' but that does not tell the full story. The name is most likely to do with the shape of the summit area, a grassy knoll surrounded by steep, rocky approaches. It could also be from holm, a nod to former settlements below the northern slope in the fertile flatlands around the River Arkaig in Glen Pean.

By the time we reached the foot of the ridge, Robert appeared to have forgotten how much he had enjoyed his first night trip. Steps in the grass lead ever upward, with no respite in the incline, and it was a slow, complaining trudge – and then we saw the summit.

To Robert's dismay, however, it was a long way off from where he believed our goal to be, almost another hour away over an up-and-down grassy highway. Every time we glimpsed the summit, it seemed to have drifted further away. I suspected he was falling out of love with this fast. However, when we finally trundled up to one of the most welcome pile of rocks we had ever seen, the sun had made an appearance, the temperature was rising fast and all was well again. It was time for a well-earned lie down and a bite to eat.

Being a keen photographer, this was heaven for Robert. The route on to Sgurr nan Coireachan has many rises and falls over minor summits but these were hardly noticed now as the views down to Loch Shiel on one side and the Arkaig hills on the other kept his camera clicking.

Coireachan, as it suggests, is a 'peak of corries'. It is also a rough peak, bare rock showing on every surface like a bad rash of dark measles. Maybe if you squinted down into the corrie at the same spot long enough the dots would start to form a picture, like those optical illusion puzzles.

The heat was now stifling, and it was wise to rest for half-an-hour here to make the most of the sunshine before we took the long, twisting route down.

Six days later, Robert and I were on the go again. We had had a heavy night at work with Scotland inevitably bowing out of Euro 96 despite beating Switzerland 1-0. Another glorious football failure. It seemed fitting that we were heading for an Alpine-like consolation.

This time the destination was Laggan Dam and the two Munros at Roughburn, Beinn a'Chaorainn and Beinn Teallach. The weather was less hospitable, though, and all the peaks along the road were well out of sight as the clouds churned menacingly as we travelled up through Glen Coe and Fort William.

Beinn a'Chaorainn is a mountain with a ferocious winter reputation, mainly because its three peaks are divided by deep bites in the ridge line which hold cornices well into the year. They are a death trap for the unwary or confused and there have been fatalities on this hill.

One famous story tells of a mountain rescue team called out by a walker to look for his friend who had fallen through a cornice. When the team located him, happily not much the worse for his ordeal, they also found another walker and a dog that had fallen through in separate incidents.

There was little chance of that today, however, just the prospect of a five-hour walk round two mountains with the chance that the low cloud would stick with us like glue all the way. Our first task was to find the little marker cairn which takes you from the track up a muddy firebreak through the forest and on to the open hillside.

Once on open ground, it was just a plod north up damp rock and grass on ever-steepening slopes, with nothing to see ahead apart from more mist. It remained that way right to the south top, on to the main summit, and then finally the north top. It was mid-June and warm, yet we were still wearing hats and gloves and our fleeces were covered in that fine mist which soaks you.

From the North Top we headed down to the col at the head of the Allt a'Chaorainn, where there is a huge marker cairn. We decided brunch would be a good idea here as this was the first time we could see more than 100 yards or so. After 10 minutes it was back up into the mist on the stony north-east ridge of Beinn Teallach and, about 40 minutes later, we were at the summit.

The views finally started to appear after we dropped down the south ridge, but the main summits were still hidden. It was disappointing, but in one way it was good – it was probably a reality check for Robert. So far it had been all sunshine and cheers when he had come out overnight. This would show whether he was in it for the long run.

Five days later we were passing the ghostly shell of Ruthven Barracks just after swinging off the A9 on our way to Glen Feshie. By 2.30am we were ready to start the march up Mullach Clach a' Bhlair and Sgor Gaoith, with another new recruit. Evelyn had been talking for a while about going up the hills but presumably Robert's nocturnal tales had proved too much. She had to try this for herself.

We headed south from our parking spot at Achlean, passing the little farm en route to the massive Coire Garbhlach by the time the sun starting rising. Evy certainly did not lack enthusiasm and she was bounding up the thick heather slopes as if it were a sprint. Robert and I were more circumspect, knowing how hard the day could be, so we had a word. You should always listen to old guys, even if you cannot understand what they are saying.

Once we were halfway up the right-hand side of the corrie we found the track that leads all the way to the first Munro summit. But we topped out on the plateau where everything was shrouded in cloud and, despite being on a substantial track, the compass and map came out to make sure we were not heading off into the swamps that cover large areas around this peak.

Happy that we were still heading where we wanted to go, we strode on, but the mist seemed to be thickening so I volunteered to go on ahead to check out the lie of the land. Just as I reached the Mullach cairn, and with Robert and Evy still in sight, the cloud started sinking and the Cairngorm peaks started to show one by one, like a burlesque dancer peeling away her misty veils. First on stage was mighty Braeriach, then we stood in silence to watch each of the mountain tops take its bow in turn, the stars of one of the longest-running shows on the circuit.

The summit of 'the stone of the plain' may not be anyone's favourite hill but it had provided us with a show of beauty that would be hard to top on any mountain. It was so bright that the whole landscape looked covered in a pale wash. The only colour was provided by Evy's gear, a riot of reds, pinks, blues and yellows.

Sgor Gaoith was now opened up and it stayed in the eyeline for the four-mile, high-level stroll over easy ground. It is a spectacular summit, a little cairn perched on the edge of high, broken cliffs which look down into the long and lonely glacial trough that holds Loch Einich. From western approaches, Sgurr Gaoith hides its secrets well. It is just a long pull up a continuous slope which never seems to end, until it suddenly comes to a shuddering halt with the massive drop into unrivalled scenery.

The one thing Sgurr Gaoith, 'the peak of wind', had not delivered so far was wind. There was hardly a breath, just enough at one stage to blow in briefly a faint mist which added to the feeling of the three of us being above the rest of the world. It was one of the most beautiful mornings I have ever had the joy of experiencing in the hills.

No-one wanted to go down. We had a snowball fight under a blazing sun 3,500 feet up a mountain while most of Scotland was in bed.

Evy would admit many years later that such a special day almost spoiled the mountains for her. The inversion, the heatwave, the high-level breakfast, the snowball fights; she doubted if she would ever savour a day like that again.

6
Scoop the Dog

IT WAS MIDNIGHT AND I was heading up the long and winding road from the A9 to lonely Rannoch railway station, a journey of nearly 36 miles. The two mountains in my line of fire were Carn Dearg and Sgor Gaibhre, which overlook Loch Ossian. But I was planning to do them in a horseshoe from the other side, by parking just short of the station and following in the steps of Scots throughout history on the Road to the Isles.

It was the off-season for football so we were finishing earlier. The spotlight was all on the Open golf championship and the news from there was usually wrapped up by around 9pm. This year it was in Lytham and the biggest tale was the threat of the caddies going on strike because they had been asked to base themselves in a former fish-and-chip van. You'd think they would have been pleased with all those good chips, but it reinforces my theory that nobody is ever truly happy.

The weather all over the country was perfect, clear and still, with a moon that meant there was never total darkness, so I was able to park up and head straight out at 1.30am.

Carn Dearg was the first objective and, after a decent track for the first couple of miles, it was straight up on to the grass-and-heather slopes to my right. The cooling breeze was a welcome climbing partner as I headed up towards the ridgeline. By the time I reached it, the light was up and the views onward unrestricted.

I had not been out for nearly four weeks because of a family break in Florida. The kids had a great time in Disney World but this was my Magic Kingdom now, one without huge queues, fast food and giant rodents wanting to shake your hand – though if Mickey appeared at this moment, I suppose I could always file it away as another case of hallucinations brought on by sleep deprivation.

This spur on to Carn Dearg, 'the red hill', is a long one but the underfoot conditions make for fast walking. As I got closer to my first target of the day, I noticed some female deer standing a few hundred yards away to my left, watching me but motionless. This was unusual as most times they will take off to a safer vantage point when anyone approaches.

But the closer I got the more they held their line. I was now more than slightly curious and stopped to have a look round. I must have been standing among the rocks for about 30 seconds when suddenly, from right underneath me, a tiny, spindly-legged figure rose and started to stumble across the hillside.

He had been lying perfectly still, beautifully camouflaged among the rocks while danger approached. His mum had been hanging about close by with the rest of the herd, keeping an eye on me.

Their plan had almost worked perfectly. I never saw the baby but my trajectory had taken me right on top of him and it was enough to panic the beast into making a dash for it.

This really was the Magic Kingdom, and Bambi was showing on the big screen. All that was missing was a hunter with a high-powered rifle to shoot his mother and the fairytale scene would have been complete.

The view from the beehive cairn on the summit of Carn Dearg is magnificent and with the perfect light at 3.30am, the whole of Glen Coe and the Nevis range stood proud in a blue wash of varying shades on the endless horizon. Even in the best weather it's never usually warm enough at that time of the day to sit around for any length of time but this was an exception. I must have spent around half an hour up there and it still wasn't nearly enough.

The walk over the pass, the Mam Ban, which separates the mountains is a bit of a bog trot and it is always with relief that you reach the summit of Sgor Gaibhre, a short, gravelly platform which provides great views of the Alder mountains. The better descent is the long, contorted ridge south which leads over the Corbett of Beinn Pharlagain but beware – in thick weather this is notorious for leading walkers astray.

Getting lost is an occupational hazard for anyone going out on the mountains. Don't listen to the guys who say it shouldn't happen. Most experienced guides I know admit to going astray every once in a while. Over-confidence is just as big a factor as inexperience, the main difference is that the experienced mountain walker can get himself out of the mess far more easily.

I learned by trial and error at first. Since then, I have taken navigational courses and winter skills training, but that is no guarantee things won't go wrong.

One of the best mountaineers I knew was notorious for going out for the occasional yomp without map or compass, and twice it went belly-up for him, once when he nearly plunged to his death in thick mist. No-one even knew he had gone out, never mind where he was.

I always reckon that getting it wrong every so often is no bad thing. It gives you a good boot up the backside and reminds you that while the hills are fun, they can be deadly for those who do not show the proper respect.

Touch wood, I have never required assistance of any sort during my night sorties. But I reckon that if the mountain rescue guys had to be called out for me, it would be one of their better gigs. Think about it. If they are called out to an incident involving someone walking during the day, it will be early evening before they start their search, though more likely it would be an overnight operation. If they were called out for me, however, then by the time I was reported missing or overdue, it would be about 10am. It's a day shift for them. I might even get club card points for being such a considerate customer.

Despite all the safety messages and information available, there are still people wandering about in the hills who do not have a clue. They are accidents waiting to happen.

There are the ones who wander about with the best of gear and gadgets but who really don't know which glen, which mountain or even which country they are in.

There are the guys who find something to moan about no matter where they are. For instance, the character we met in a bothy in Knoydart sitting reading a book. We discovered he had travelled from the south of England but then thought it was "a bit too cloudy" to go up any mountains.

And then there are the out-and-out lunatics. Most of the time they are looking to tag along with you. Even if you told them you were heading up the glen to top yourself they would still tell you that sounded like a good idea and ask to come along.

Some might add that there are occasionally some crazed-looking souls who wander about the mountains at night, but I have to say I have never noticed that.

Fergus, in particular, does not suffer fools gladly. One day when we were sitting on the summit of Beinn Dorain, we were surprised to see two guys arriving from the other side of the hill. Like most other walkers, we had come up by the tourist route which starts from Bridge of Orchy, at the railway station.

Dorain is a massive lump, rising up like a huge rock surfing wave when it first looms into view as you head north on the A82 from Tyndrum, so fair play to the lads for having charged up the south ridge. It's a steep pull with not much respite.

One of them had one of the biggest packs we had ever seen. From it, he extracted what looked like an industrial tea urn and started to get a brew going. How much tea could two men drink?

Soon it was obvious they did not have a clue where they were. Maybe the south ridge was not a deliberate choice after all. Maybe they thought they were on the road to the National History Museum. "Which peak is this?" was the quote that gave it away. They were eccentrics all right, although Fergus cut to the chase – he christened them the Dick Brothers.

"Who in their right mind would come up that ridge if they didn't have to?" he asked.

"Maybe they stopped for a caramel slice down the road and are still so traumatised by the price they've lost their minds."

"Shut up."

The Dicks were busy studying their map and trying to pinpoint their location. Then one of them pointed eastwards towards Loch Lyon. "What's that water?"

His compadre looked intently at the map for a few more seconds then said: "I think it's Loch Lee-on."

I turned to Fergus and said: "Jesus, I think we must have stumbled into France."

We left the Dick Brothers and their samovar and headed to Beinn an Dothaidh, which was just back over the border from France. We didn't see them again. They are probably still wandering the hills, downing tea by the gallon, blissfully unaware of any apparent danger.

Madmen, perhaps, but every so often you meet someone who should not be out on their own, never mind anywhere near a mountain. Ladies and gentlemen, I give you: The Mud Man.

Fergus, Malcolm and I ran into this gentleman when we were parked at Loch Moraig near Blair Atholl as we prepared to do the three Munros of Beinn a'Ghlo.

While we were getting changed, this guy appeared on foot from out of nowhere and started to chat. He was wee and skinny, with the rat-faced appearance of a heroin addict. He told us he had recently started working at a hotel in Pitlochry and had decided to get out and do a bit of walking. But there was no sign of how he had got here and he did not look well-equipped or fit.

"What are you planning to do then?" I asked.

"Well, what are you planning to do?" he replied.

Oh-oh, danger. When someone asks that, you know they have not made a plan and are hoping to hook up. Ten minutes later and we would be getting a hard luck story and an appeal for cash.

"Well, we're heading up there but we're going to be moving fast," said Fergus. In other words: Sod off. Picking up the vibe, he turned and waved his arm off to the right where there was a boggy morass filled with reeds and lying water. "I think I'll go over there."

We thought he meant he was going to walk in that direction, not go into the swamp, so we parted ways. In hindsight, we should have tied him up securely and left him at the car park until the relevant authorities could get him.

Beinn a'Ghlo is a mini-mountain range and covers a huge area. One old stalker's legend says there are 19 corries and that a rifle could be fired in any one of them and the report not heard in another. Handy to know if you are thinking of setting up a terrorist camp.

The rocky scar up the front of Carn Liath – in some places it's more like walking in a trench – takes you on to the ridge in good time and, once there, all thoughts of our curious encounter with the Mud Man disappeared.

From the summit of the grey one, it's a twisting but obvious way on to the much higher second peak of the round, the wonderfully titled Braigh Coire Chruinn-bhalgain, 'the upland of the corrie of the round blisters'. A sharp turn to the right leads up to the boulder-strewn summit ridge of the final peak, Carn nan Gobhar, another spot for goat lovers.

The journey home goes to the equally rocky peak of silver, Airgiod

Bheinn, and then straight down off the end of the ridge to pick up a path through the waterlogged and bog-strewn ground round the edge of the mountain. It was an exercise in bog dodging and it was mainly successful, the only casualty being the redoubtable Scoop. He had been skipping over the boggy ground off the path when he suddenly sank into a deep patch of watery mud up to his chin. He struggled out of the glaur almost shame-faced as we guffawed. He then tucked his head down and ran away.

"What's up with him?" I asked.

"Oh, he'll be in the huff. He doesn't like people laughing at him," replied Malcolm.

That was a new one. I already knew a lot of Scoop's dislikes, one of which was members of HM Constabulary, thanks to an incident once on our way back down the Loch Lomond road.

We were heading back to Glasgow when we were flagged down by a cop warning us of a hold-up further down the road. When he leaned down to speak to Malcolm the dog went crazy, barking and snarling, trying to get through the window at the officer.

"What's the problem with him?" he asked Malcolm.

Cue the worst reply ever. "Eh, he doesn't like hats."

As we drove off, Fergus asked: "He doesn't like hats?"

"It was the first thing I could think of. I could hardly say I trained him to growl at cops, could I?"

Shortly after Scoop's mud bath huff, we arrived back at the cars where I noticed a figure about half a mile away. There was something just not quite right about it.

"What the hell is that?" I asked.

Fergus took a look and said: "It looks like a guy putting up fence posts."

Another look suggested that could be right. The guy was lifting up what looked like a fence post and then putting it down into the ground.

"Why would you put fence posts up in a bog?" asked Malcolm.

We watched for a while and then it clicked – this person was stuck in the bog, and every time he pulled one leg out, the other would sink. So he repeated the process: one leg out, one leg sinks; one leg out, one leg sinks.

However, he was making progress and about 10 minutes later he managed to reach the end of the bog and came out to the car park. The figure that approached us now had mud caked up to his waist, and his face and upper torso were spattered with it. Here was the guy we had met seven hours ago – had he been in this bog ever since?

He could hardly speak after his efforts. He just came and sat beside us.

"Good day?" we asked.

"Naw, got into a bit of mess."

Fergus was trying his best not to get involved. He had decided the guy was of the looney tunes variety. He was also very proud of his car, a VW Golf, and kept it immaculate. We had already said our goodbyes and, as Fergus got into his car, the Mud Man asked: "Any chance of a lift to Pitlochry?"

Fergus just looked at the mud-spattered mess for a few seconds and then said: "Not in my car there isn't." And sped off.

Malcolm and I were struggling not to fall about laughing but we could not leave him. I offered to take him with us but, five minutes down the road, we realised that Fergus's loony radar had been spot on. As we neared Pitlochry, I asked the Mud Man where he wanted to be dropped.

"Where are you guys going?" was the reply.

"We're going to Glasgow. We start work at five."

"Hmmm. Think I might come with you, if that's all right."

"I don't think so. You're getting out here."

My next outing was a great example of how things can go wrong and how you can turn them into a positive.

Robert and I were back in Glen Feshie, heading up the Coire

Fhearnagan path from Achlean at 2.30am to climb Monadh Mor and Beinn Bhrotain. This route involves a crossing of the Moine Mhor, a huge featureless expanse of moss, grass and bog with few markers.

It was stiflingly warm and the mist was a diaphanous curtain down to the floor of the glen. Although the track to the plateau is clear even in the dark, you need good compass work when you reach the top of it and head on to the plateau.

We had taken our readings to the little Loch nan Cnapan and were also hoping the mist would start to lift and give us a helping hand. On the way we diverted slightly to reach Tom Dubh, a nearby Munro Top, and then we planned to pick up the earlier route on to Monadh Mor.

We appeared to be on target but the walk seemed to be going on and on without any noticeable rise in the contours. After about an hour and with no visibility, I began to think we may have got it wrong. Then the ground started rising and our confidence returned. But again, after another half hour or so, it seemed the distances we were covering were too much. Either we were going really slowly or we had gone off course. But once again, we breathed a sigh of relief when a good path appeared going in the right direction.

About 20 minutes later, the path took us to a cliff edge, then joined another path going north to south. Decision time – as far as the map showed, there were no cliffs on Monadh Mor and no path was marked there either. We decided to head north first, following the path along the line of the cliffs.

Eventually we came to a cairn, but this was not Monadh Mor and the ground then started to go down again slightly. It was time to turn south to see if we could have better luck.

Again the ground was rising, so we stuck with it. After all, if there is still a slope ahead then you haven't yet hit the highest point. Next up was a boulder field. We tiptoed our way between the grey, haphazardly piled rocks until we reached a big cairn.

According to the map, this was not Monadh Mor. Four hours

should have seen us to the summit comfortably. We had now been going way longer than that and still had not touched down. The map was providing few clues. Sometimes the older OS ones may be lacking some features, but the real puzzle was that the compass was still telling us we had been going in the right direction.

It was time for a break and a morning cuppa. As we sat like two blindfolded men considering our options, the clouds blew away almost instantly to reveal our position. We were not on the top of Monadh Mor; we were at the pointed summit of Sgor an Lochain Uaine – almost three miles away.

We had crossed the shoulder of Monadh Mor in the mist and ended up on the edge of Braeriach's massive rock amphitheatre, An Garbh Choire. The little green body of water hundreds of feet below, Lochain Uaine, gives this peak its name although it is often referred to as The Angel's Peak, most likely to balance the presence of The Devil's Point further south on the ridge. We were now getting the feeling that the angels were on our side for once in this walk.

The distances involved in reaching the heart of the Cairngorms are usually immense and our adjustments to confirm our position had succeeded only in leading us further astray. But now that we knew where we were, we couldn't just pull the plug. Cairn Toul was close and with only a 600-foot climb to its short, level summit ridge, it would have been crazy to leave it for another day. Now we would still end up with two ticks for the day, just not the ones we had set off to do.

The only trouble was that by the time we had topped Cairn Toul we would have quite a few more miles under our belts than we had originally intended and it was a long way back. Instead of an eight-hour walk, it had turned into nearly 12.

I was well on target on my charge to the finish. But the failure to reach Monadh Mor and Beinn Bhrotain was still nagging away.

I'm not good with unfinished business, so I suppose it was inevitable that just one week later I was driving up the A9 to

Newtonmore, then following the winding road past the ruins of Ruthven Barracks into Glen Feshie for another assault on the two that got away.

I set off again up the Coire Fhearnagan path in the 4am darkness with my head torch shining ahead, more like a comfort blanket than a necessity as the moonlight was picking the way ahead quite clearly. It was still dark by the time I reached Loch nan Cnapan at the far end of the Moine Mhor. The mountains we had accidentally ended up on last time were just black silhouettes on the skyline ahead, with the sky a deep shade of purple with pink and yellow patches swirling through. The little lochan was like a miniature version of the sky, the reflection from above providing the only light in a seemingly endless plateau of darkness.

Tom Dubh was carefully ignored this time, but as I started ascending the slopes of Monadh Mor on a south-easterly line, the clarity of the morning was quickly changing. The higher I went the thicker the mist was becoming. Surely I couldn't get caught out with these hills again?

I couldn't shake the thought that this could be another failure, as I plodded onwards, ever uphill with nothing in sight. I was thinking that if I missed out again I would just retreat to the car and drive off towards the horizon. I could not go back to work if I failed. I would have to find a service revolver and do the decent thing – shoot as many B-list celebrities as possible.

The multi-coloured beauty of the sky was now long forgotten as I kept to my compass line. All thoughts of a sunshine-bathed day out in the hills had vanished. Reaching the summits was now all that mattered. There are no soaring rock faces on this approach to Monadh Mor, just a constant gentle rise over tundra-like grass, gravel and rock. There is hardly a hint that you are nearing the top of a peak 3,651 feet above sea level.

After more than three-and-a-half hours' walking, the mist started thinning and I emerged into the sunshine above another cloud inversion. It's amazing how a little decent weather lifts the spirits and within a few minutes the summit of Monadh Mor was in sight. It had only taken the best part of three weeks, but I was there.

The gap between Monadh Mor and Beinn Bhrotain is not too deep and the walk along the short, grass-and-gravel ridge was accompanied by the views of dark fins of rock sticking through the clouds on my left, sharks in a sea of cotton wool. In the 40 minutes it took to reach the summit of 'the peak of the mastiff', the inversion had sunk farther on the left, into the heart of the Cairngorms, but was still fully intact on the right, over the whole of Perthshire.

7
Lager Than Life

ONE OF THE GREATEST pleasures of a hard day in the hills is the thought of a foaming pint waiting for you at the bar on your return. Never mind the fact that alcohol isn't the best aid to dehydration, most walkers and climbers just can't wait to sink one as soon as they hit sea level again.

On some long, hard walks, it can be one of the things that keeps you going. Many a time I have walked or, more likely, stumbled my way back to the car with an invisible pint dangling in front of my eyes tantalisingly out of reach, a liquid carrot on a stick for the hillwalking donkey.

In a previous life I joined a group from work who went running on country roads. Five or six miles, twice a week. I didn't particularly want to run, but it was a way of keeping fit. The guy who organised the runs was a very serious runner. One night after an eight-mile circuit, a few of us stopped off at the pub on the way home and started getting in about the pints. Our real runner was horrified.

"What's the point of drinking four or five pints after all that exercise? That's just defeating the purpose."

"No, that is the purpose. We've exercised so that we can go out drinking."

We would remain at odds on that one.

The Scots, the Irish and those climbers from the northern parts of England tend to share that philosophy. It's a pint, nothing more, nothing less. Those from further south are more inclined towards a half-pint. And the Welsh? Well, they are more of a mystery, but they mainly sing about drink and, to be fair, they do carry a tune well. But that's another story.

We were in the middle of an autumn heatwave and it would have been foolish to have let it go without taking advantage. So I drove towards Glen Shiel with Radiohead as the soundtrack, *No Surprises* serving as a hopeful sign. The Five Sisters are a tourist board delight, soaring peaks which rise in regimented steps along a muscular but beautiful ridge that runs from midway down Glen Shiel to the head of Loch Duich. They are as recognisable a pile of bumps as the Loch Ness Monster and the view of them from the top of the Pass of Ratagan is on postcards all round the world.

The problem I faced was doing it solo. That meant leaving my car at one end of the ridge and hitching back along the road or, God forbid, walking. It's a long way.

The other option was a circuit from Morvich at the head of the loch, walking up the track in Gleann Lichd to the bothy then taking a direct line south to reach the col between the nearby Brothers ridge and the Sisters and then following the ridge back over all the summits to the start.

That is also a long day, but I felt it was the better option rather than relying on the kindness of passing motorists. I had learned from previous experience that bagging a lift can prove harder than bagging the hills. I also feel uneasy asking someone to let a half-crazed looking, mud-caked stranger into their car. Kindness is often repaid by having their vehicle stink for the rest of their journey, or by having animal shit ingrained in their floor for weeks afterward.

I still feel sorry for a lovely old couple who stopped to give Malcolm a lift after we had descended the South Shiel Ridge. After many failed attempts to get picked up, he was shown pity by the pensioners who stopped in their brand new car. As he got into the car he heard the pointed end of his ice axe, which was attached to his rucksack, rip through the fabric of their roof. They never noticed and he was too mortified to mention it. No good deed ever goes unpunished.

The track from Morvich is easy enough in darkness and in an hour or so I had reached the bothy, the rather grandly named Gleann Lichd House. I remember looking at this on a map and thinking it would be an extravagant, posh pile of bricks belonging to a reclusive millionaire. It was only when members of my climbing club mentioned having to take sleeping bags and firewood that I realised this was not the case.

The sun had risen and I had built up a fair head of sweat. By the time I had struggled up to the Bealach an Lapain almost two hours later I was almost out of fluid. That would prove to be a problem in the hours ahead but, for now, all I was concerned about was the amazing view into Glen Shiel.

The first peak on the circuit, Sgurr nan Spainteach – 'the peak of the Spaniards' – is not one of the Five Sisters. The name comes from the circumstances surrounding the Battle of Glen Shiel in 1715, when Spanish mercenaries fighting for Bonnie Prince Charlie were forced to retreat over the mountain after the ground they were on caught fire in the face of the firepower of the English muskets from below. With the heat on the ridge, I was beginning to imagine how they must have felt.

The next peak, Sgurr nan Ciste Duibhe, is the first Sister and the first Munro. It is 'the peak of the black chest' and, with Spanish mercenaries running all over this area, it is understandable that the object in question could refer to treasure aboard one of the galleons on which they had arrived. The real explanation is more mundane and refers to a deep hollow on the south-west slopes of the hill.

There is a little climb down a rocky front here, then a kink in the ridge that could lead the unwary off course. On a day of mist and moisture, I once came across a guy here who was leading a party of women along the ridge. He had his Ordnance Survey (OS) map fully spread out – always a worrying sign – and, when he spotted me, asked: "Excuse me, could you tell which hill this is?"

They had come together as part of an online walking club. It was no surprise that when we met up again, further on, the ladies asked me if I could escort them off the mountain. "I don't think he knows what he's doing," one of them whispered to me. Ah, the perils of internet dating.

The ridge starts curving round to the right and next up is the recently promoted Munro Sgurr na Carnach. 'The peak of the stony ground' is a simple but effective description. The Five Sisters is a ridge that seems to attract the confused. Here was a guy who looked as if he had just crawled out of the Sahara. Maybe that would have been easier than the route he'd taken – he had come straight up the unrelentingly steep west ridge of Sgurr Fhuaran from the main road by mistake and now he was not sure where he was. I didn't like to have to break the news to him. The pain was clear on his face when he realised he would now have to go back along the main ridge and then retrace his steps the whole way before starting again if he wanted to bag all the peaks.

My day as a tour guide wasn't finished. Sgurr Fhuaran, the highest peak on the ridge and the steepest, was next. After a stiff pull-up through the rock-strewn slopes, I met a very polite chap from Peterborough called Neil. We got chatting and it appeared he would be happier with some company for the rest of the traverse. Next thing we were new best buddies and heading along to the end of the ridge.

The final Sister, Sgurr na Moraich, is not a Munro, but it is a big, steep hill and the descent to Morvich is a real knee-breaker and seems never-ending. By the time we reached the bottom I was suffering badly from dehydration. I had to have drink – and lots of it. The little emergency juice I had in the car was not nearly enough. I mentioned I would be stopping at the Cluanie Inn for a refreshment, so Neil said he would get the drinks in. I asked for a lager and lime.

I had assumed that it would be a pint of the golden liquid. In this case, it should have been apparent that a gallon would be more appropriate judging by my state. But our friends in the deep south have a different take and I arrived to find a half-pint of lager and lime on the table.

My disappointment must have been immediately obvious, as Neil said: "Oh, were you wanting a pint?" He was already heading back to the bar. Cheers, mate.

It was drink that had reignited my early affair with the hills. Some 15 years after my scout adventures, the opportunity arose to venture out again. One of my wife's cousins used to go on backwoods weekends with some of his friends and they invited me along. Mostly it was an excuse to have a weekend somewhere different which involved drinking a lot with the occasional walk thrown in. One of the guys was quite into it, and I suspect that's where the walking part came in. The rest of us were into the drinking part.

Most times it involved camping. I have never been a great fan of camping. That may sound strange coming from someone who spends wild nights out in the mountains, but I just can't be bothered with it.

The amount of preparation to set up, pack up and then leave again drives me daft. I prefer to travel light. A bivvy bag was good enough for many years, although I have now moved upmarket to a super-duper sleeping bag which doubles as a tent. It has a mere four pegs and is as light as a fleece, so it stays in the rucksack and can be called into action at any time.

I was also told by the person who sold me it that I could sleep in a river all night and not get wet. He said nothing about drowning, though. I haven't tested that out and I'm not sure I ever will.

Strangely, I remember little of the mountains we climbed. Or perhaps when you consider how much alcohol was consumed it is not really surprising.

The first weekend trip was to Oban. I was a city boy. I had never been over to the west coast hills before and after we had left Perth behind the journey took on that feeling of being in uncharted territory, a true voyage of discovery.

The slow but beautiful road wound through peaceful villages and towns that had been just names on a map to me – Methven, Gilmerton, Comrie, St Fillans – then brushed the shores of Loch Earn, where water sports enthusiasts flocked round its edges in various stages of activity, before turning up through Glen Ogle to reach the road to Crianlarich.

Next, the mountains started thrusting their way into the equation – the mighty twins Ben More and Stob Binnein, with its sawn-off cap, then the double-pronged Ben Lui and its satellites – as we made our way into what appeared to be the last frontier of civilisation, Tyndrum.

The dramatic sweep of Beinn Dorain was next to fill the windscreen, the evening's dying sunlight illuminating it like the guardian to the gates of Hell. Up through Glen Coe, and my first encounter with the mountain that was to form such a large part of my mountaineering years, Buachaille Etive Mor.

Here was a real mountain, a terrifying pyramid of Alpine grandeur, nothing like the huge but mainly grassy peaks we had so far passed. And the little figures buzzing all-round the base of it, wrapped in ropes and climbing metal; these were real mountaineers, not the backpack-carrying ramblers straggling their way up the West Highland Way, alongside the road.

This was the formative moment of my hill life. Here was the

world I wanted to be part of.

Travelling through the pass of Glen Coe at any time is a pleasure. It is a place to suit all moods. Sun, snow, rain, mist, there is always something special to take from the journey. It is often at its best in swirling cloud, tempting glimpses of its treasures and brutal history coming into view and then, just as quickly, fading away again.

By the time we had swung round on the way to Oban, the weather had turned, and it was time for my favourite activity – putting up a tent in a monsoon. If we had stayed in the car we would have been dry. But we were here to camp, so camp we did, although we were so wet by the time we crawled under canvas that I suspect sleeping outside would not have been any worse.

It sounded like we were sheltering under a waterfall. Unconsciousness came soon, however, no doubt helped by strong drink, and the feeling of being a human sponge was doubly endorsed.

Brilliant sunlight and the chorus of birdsong you hear only after the passing of a storm awoke us, and a quick recce outside the tent revealed the mist-wreathed waters of the Lynn of Lorne, a ferry silently gliding through the glassy surface, gently making its way into harbour. After breakfast (another tick on my camping hate list – slow, messy and always tasteless), it was time to wash up, pack and head for the hills.

We were going up Ben Cruachan, a huge mountain in the Pass of Brander. Cruachan is of vital importance to the hydro-electric industry and tourists can be driven into the centre of the vast, hollowed-out mountain to see the wonders for themselves. When the Queen officially opened the facility in 1965, her cortege swept into the heart of the mountain. Trust the royals to do the Munros the easy way.

It takes seven or eight hours to go round all the peaks that make up the Cruachan horseshoe. However, because of all the messing about with tents, it was now mid-afternoon and the plan was to get so far up and then, horror of horrors, camp again. Hangovers, lack of fitness and the carrying of what seemed like tons of camping equipment got us only as far as the minor peak of Meall Cuanaill, where we decided to set up camp.

It was a beautiful spot, but my fellow campers seemed to take more joy in the act of putting up and taking down the tent than in actually ever getting anywhere. Perhaps a dead adder in their bags would have speeded things up. We sat in the silent darkness, watching a light bobbing ever upwards along the ridge above us, a lone walker heading for the summit of Cruachan.

It is hard to believe that in the years ahead I would be that lone figure, pushing onwards into the dark.

The following morning we woke to driving rain and high winds, so we packed up, dropped down to the road, then went home. A three-day expedition to not climb a hill. Brilliant.

We had three or four other outings but, apart from an expedition up a snowy Ben Nevis, it was not until I started climbing hills seriously 10 years later that I figured out where I had been during those trips. I remembered every single, miserable moment of the camping, though.

Mid-September is one of my favourite times for walking. The oppressive heat and wildly variant rainfall of the summer is on its way out and there is often a more benign feeling to the weather. It is also getting darker in the mornings, so the decision is whether to start at the same time or to have a lie-in – that is, an hour's rest in the car before setting off.

Since we were heading for Glen Nevis, Robert and I decided to leave later, around 3am, and make a leisurely journey to the car park at the road-end in the glen. We set off in the dark to head up Nevis Gorge but, by the time we had threaded our way up on the path above the deep chasm of roaring waters and reached the flat grasslands near Steall Bridge, the sun was fully up.

We followed the track along the Water of Nevis then left it at the ruined Steall cottage. The track becomes very stony and then degenerates into a muddy path, which eventually leads through to Loch Treig and the remote Corrour station, a true wilderness route.

Instead we were heading steeply north-east up the ridge to Sgurr a'Bhuic, the first peak on the circuit to Aonach Beag. The high-level route then goes over Stob Coire Bhealaich and up rockier ground to the 4,000-foot Munro summit. Keeping you company all the way is the view down to the intimidating cliffs.

The vistas all the way up over the Mamores and the Nevis range are panoramic, but there was a sea of dark cloud just caressing the tops and the highest summits were hidden. At the Aonach Beag cairn there was no view. Once again, we were thwarted by early-morning mist for the last few hundred feet, a constant bane at this time of the day.

An hour or so later, as we headed down from the circuit, it blew away completely to uncover a stunning portrait of Ben Nevis and the Carn Mor Dearg arete, a spectacular bouldery tightrope, huge walls of rock curving gracefully round to the highest place in Britain. It was the ideal spot for lunch, the mighty Ben seen from one of its better sides.

The forecast was wet and windy for the following Wednesday, then calm for Wednesday night and Thursday morning, before a huge storm was moving in around lunchtime. If I timed it right, I could set off in the early hours, do a couple of peaks and be back at the car before all hell broke loose. The trick was not to be too ambitious, so I decided on a bit of tidying up.

The Cairngorms were ideal – good paths and not too horrendous a journey – so I headed for Braemar and the starting point for so many classic walks, the Linn of Dee.

As I got out of the car, the force of the wind became apparent. The whole forest was moving as one, a huge collective sigh from the swaying trees as they bent to the will of the wind. Although it was dark, the clear sky was giving off plenty of light and as yet there was no sign of rain as I headed into the woods en route to Derry

Lodge, about four miles along the track. I was planning to climb Carn a'Mhaim and Derry Cairngorm, so it was off up the Lairig an Laoigh, one of the two passes that divide the Cairngorm massif into three sections.

As I headed further up the pass, the wind picked up and the cloud started rolling in. By the time I had reached the Hutchison Memorial Hut, the open shelter in Coire Etchachan which has the air and positioning of an Alpine refuge, visibility was zero and it was cold and damp. The high walls of this natural amphitheatre were darkening. Still, I reckoned I could do one of the peaks.

As I headed further up through a boulder field, conditions deteriorated by the minute and with the wind in my face it was becoming hard to walk. Now the plan changed. I figured it was simpler to forget Derry Cairngorm and go to the summit of Ben Macdui, then take a line down to Carn a'Mhaim and out by the other track, the Lairig Ghru.

The only glimpses of landscape were the massive cliffs on my left, huge bites out of the ridgeline, and soon I was at the huge summit cairn. I took my readings and headed off for Carn a'Mhaim, a long, long way below. Within 20 minutes I was back at the Macdui cairn after becoming confused in wet, mossy ground. Despite holding my reading – or thinking I had – I had come round in a circle. As I sheltered at the cairn, I decided I'd had enough of a battering. My good luck had taken me back to Macdui. I should cash in now and get off the hill.

So much for the storm window. Eight hours in the dark, cold and wet, and I had achieved nothing except a reminder that I could get myself out of bother.

It was a reminder that no matter how much time and effort you invest in a plan, sometimes shit happens. The next overnight assault proved that.

Early October, and I was gearing up for a long trip. I was heading to Glen Affric to do Toll Creagach and Tom a'Choinich. The walk round the two mountains would take about five-and-a-half hours – the return journey up the A9 via Inverness would take about seven-and-a-half, more if traffic was heavy on the way back.

By the time it came to set off in the car I had thoughts of abandoning the venture. I had not been feeling well all day in the office due to an upset stomach.

I blame the staff canteen. The chef had an obsession with sausages. It seemed he had a sausage mountain. So we got steak and sausage pie. Sausage casserole. Liver and sausage. Pasta and sausage. There was even sausage in the lasagne. He was truly the Marco Pierre White of sausagery. On this occasion, I think it was the apple and sausage crumble which had done me in.

The weather was good and the chance to get another walk under my belt proved too alluring, so I turned to that cure-all for tummy upsets – Guinness. Yes, a pint of the black gold would settle things down, bring back the solidity to your stomach. After all, Guinness is good for you.

One swift pint later and I was off. The Guinness seemed to have done the trick. I had a clear run and around 5am was parked up at the side of Loch Beinn a'Mheadhoin in Glen Affric. From there a track runs west, then north, then west again into the heart of the Affric peaks. My route involved cutting off the track just as it turned west for the second time and going straight up the relatively dull, grassy south ridge.

It was easy going and I was soon striding over the russet tufts of grass and scattered stones that lead to the trig point and cairn that mark the summit of Toll Creagach, the rocky hollow. Its name refers to a feature on the northern side of the hill and makes it sound far more dashing and romantic than it is. In reality it is a shapeless pudding, a big lump of a hill that brings you down to earth with a bump at the end of the most beautiful ridges in the area.

While the walking was comfortable, my stomach was not and by the time I had descended into the Bealach Toll Easa, emergency measures were necessary.

The bealach is a special spot for deer watchers and stalkers. Thousands of animals gather in the corrie on the north side to feed and today was no exception. But I was more interested in finding a place out of the wind pronto before I was visited by my old Welsh/Irish mate Dai O'Rea.

If only Malcolm had been here to offer his advice. He was an expert in outdoor expulsion. For some reason, soon after we started walking he would be struck by the urge to disappear into the woods. He soon became known as Forest Dump.

So it was that I found myself with trousers round my ankles, sitting with my bare bahookie protruding over a large rock as I gave vent to my troubles.

Normally you would use a small trowel to dig a hole and bury your business. But this allows for the fact that you can plan ahead. When your stomach informs you that it needs to evacuate immediately, there is no time for niceties. There was barely enough time to get free of my trousers. If I had been wearing the extra winter gear I would not have made it in time and I would have had to roll in sheep or deer crap to smell sweeter.

An outdoors toilet stop sees you produce an ever-tapering thing of beauty, a mini-Munro for the flies to enjoy scaling. But this was no Mr Whippy. I didn't need to dig a hole. There was simply nothing of any consistency to bury.

It paints a beautiful picture, does it not? A picturesque Highland landscape at 6am, hundreds of deer feeding in the morning gloom and perched above them on the ridge, a bare white arse protruding over a large rock making roaring sounds that, fortunately, some of the stags did not mistake for a rutting challenge. It would have been a great calendar pic – I could have been a poster boy for the Braveheart crowd. All I needed to do was shout "Freedom" in a strangled voice.

The year was drawing to a close and so was my enthusiasm. Most of the hills I now needed to climb were far-flung and the conditions never seemed to be conducive to long, solo trips in the middle of the night.

I did, however, manage to claim one hill which took me to the 180 mark. Geal Charn – the white hill – lies in the Monadhliath near Laggan. On a snowy Sunday morning in mid-November I decided on an early start so that I could reach the foot of the hill by first light.

When I parked up at Garva Bridge, an old humpback stone Wade bridge, there was a welcoming committee awaiting me. Hundreds of pheasants flocked to the car. They were all over the place – it was like a worldwide rally for pheasants.

I assumed they were looking for food and decided to head off sharpish before they realised they outnumbered me (pheasants seem particularly stupid, but I did not want to underestimate their arithmetical skills). As I headed north up the track, they came too. I felt like a Munro-bagging Pied Piper until they realised, just like my daughters did many years before, that it was not worth climbing a mountain just to get a bite to eat.

8
Yankee Dawdle

NO ONE CAN EVER accuse me of not doing my bit for the Scottish tourist industry. An old friend, David, who now lived in the USA, was back for a visit and had brought along a buddy from New York. He had asked if Alex could stay with me with for a few days to spare him the torture of staying with his mother-in-law. Alex wanted to sample Glasgow life.

Whisky certainly appealed to him but tartan did not, and a planned jaunt to the tourist sights of Edinburgh with David and family hardly filled him with enthusiasm.

The first night we had a session in the Ritz Bar in Charing Cross where Alex was amused by the toilet facilities. "That's the first time I've had to piss in a trough for 20 years," he announced.

The weather was good and I had been planning to go into the hills after work the next night. I told Alex he could have spare keys to my flat as I was heading off up a mountain.

"You're going climbing in the dark? Are you nuts?"

"I do it all the time, it's fine," I replied, somewhat defensively. "It's the best feeling in the world to be sitting at the top of a mountain with the sun coming up."

That obviously struck a chord because he asked: "Would I be able to do it?"

This had not been part of my plans. I thought Alex would be wanting to go on another pub tour with David and some other worthies while I continued my quest to tick off the Munros.

As he thought more and more about it, however, he became convinced that this would be a real Scottish experience. No Princes Street and castle parades for him – this was the real deal.

I still wasn't too keen. I could not do what I had planned by going out with somebody who had never been up a mountain before. On the other hand I was tired and, although I wanted to get out to feed my need, the thought of a long journey was not that appealing.

Maybe we could do something not too far away, something short and spectacular without being dangerous. Something like Buachaille Etive Mor. Perfect – everyone falls in love with the Buachaille. I've often said that if I was around 3,000 feet taller I would have been tempted to propose to it a while back.

Alex was in decent condition, albeit his fitness had been earned daily in a gym, and he did not carry any weight. I could kit him out and look after him and it would keep me ticking over fitness-wise. So, just after midnight, we made for the gates of Glen Coe and the Big Herdsman.

It was inversion weather again as we headed off into the mist, over the wooden bridge and up the path past the whitewashed cottage of Lagangarbh into the shattered landscape of Coire na Tulaich, the big bowl that fronts the northern side of the mountain.

In summer, it's a walk up through a sea of rock debris and the nearer the top of the bowl, the more the ground shifts beneath your feet. It used to be a case of two steps forward, one step back but now there is the option of a solid rock staircase taking walkers up to the right into a more stable landscape, which eases the frustration of the screes and the swearing of the participants. It was great fun on the way down, though, to launch yourself into the moving bed of rocks and ride it like a surfer on a wave, taking you down this section in minutes.

In winter, though, the Buachaille can be a killer. The walls round the corrie build up massive cornices. Huge tracts of debris filling the lower slopes and stream bed are testament to the deadly avalanche potential. The Buachaille is probably second only to Ben Nevis in its toll of fatalities.

The angle of the upward push, allied to the fact that you are protected from the worst of the winds by the massive walls encasing you, mean the ascent is hot work at any time. On a still day with hardly a breath of wind it can be a heat trap and, although it was still 3am, sweat was pouring off us.

The mist was now above and below us and the only views we had were the inside of our oven, but I was hopeful that by the time we climbed out of the corrie and on to the open ridge, there may be a breeze to cool us down as well as some views.

The topping out at the head of the corrie is a revelation in good visibility, the views opening out to the Glen Etive peaks straight ahead and the eagle's nest of the Buachaille's next peak, Stob na Doire, looming up menacingly on the right. We were not that lucky.

I've been up the Buachaille around 20 times and have seen it in all of its moods. On any other day, I would have regarded this as a sensational atmosphere, swirling cloud bubbling up from the corrie like steam from a witch's cauldron, and a sea of cloud hiding both the road below and every peak along the skyline. My disappointment in the conditions was more for my American visitor. It would be akin to someone travelling from Japan to London on the trip of a lifetime to see Big Ben and then finding it covered up for repairs. This would be Alex's one and only chance to see the mountain in its true colours, but so far we were striking out.

We now had just 20 minutes or so up to the left through reddish rocks before we hit the main peak, Stob Dearg, and the chance to have uninterrupted views of some of Scotland's finest hills. There was still no respite by the time we reached the massive cairn which sits on the edge of the eastern cliffs, almost as if suspended in mid-air, with its normally expansive views.

"Well, here it is – your first mountain peak. Sorry you can't see anything."

"Ah, forget it. Not your fault. Who expects to be on a mountain at this time anyway? Actually, it's the second time I've been up a mountain. I once went to the top of a hill in New York State. We actually drove most of the way. Got out and walked the last bit – nearly got run over by a Volkswagen at the top, would you believe."

There's a thought – if you could drive up most of the Munros, I wonder how many people would be on the hills? Instead of the usual weekend people jam on the Aonach Eagach, you could have traffic snarl-ups just slightly further down.

It's certainly the way you would imagine certain Americans doing mountains. All the way to the top of Mount Obesity in a gas-guzzler, then a 20-foot breathless plod over to the cairn, where they would pull out carry-out bags containing a couple of double cheeseburgers with fries and a super-sized milkshake. A quick call to mountain rescue to get them airlifted back to their car and that's the day complete.

Alex did not seem in any hurry to move. To my suggestion that we get him back to Glasgow, he replied: "Isn't there any more we can do here?" I couldn't decide whether he loved the experience or was trying to delay his trip to Edin-burg.

It doesn't take much to persuade me to spend more time on high, so we sauntered back along the ridge to Stob na Doire. It was now about 8am and the cloud was gradually drifting away, so going that extra mile had paid off.

We dropped down into the next corrie, heading for the Lairig Gartain, the pass at the side of the mountain that would lead us back to the car. Alex was certain he spotted an eagle perched on rocks, drinking from a stream (it was a rock, but he wanted to see an eagle so, being the good tourist guide, I told him that it was) and he lay down at one stream so that the water ran over his head and face. But the biggest surprise for him was when he reached the Lairig.

"Where are all the houses?" he asked.

"There are no houses. No-one is allowed to build here."

"Jeez, if this was back home, there would be houses all over this place." Let's hope Donald Trump and his pals were not listening.

When we got back to the car, the layby was packed with sightseers starting their day, or by other walkers thinking they were getting an early start. I said to Alex: "You know, you've probably missed Edinburgh."

He didn't look too worried. He moseyed (he was American after all) on over to two young foreign girls looking up at the Buachaille, and said: "You know, we've just climbed up there, and this guy (pointing to me) is one of Scotland's top mountain guides." As chat-up lines go, it's hard to beat.

The Buachaille has formed a pivotal part of my mountain life. It is the mountain that set it all off, the mountain that drew me into walking and climbing.

It has the shape of what a mountain should look like. From the road over Rannoch Moor it appears as a perfect pyramid of sheer rock, its buttresses, walls and gullies standing proudly, throwing out a challenge to all-comers. No soft edges, all sharp, pointed contours. No grass slopes, all chunks of sandstone and granite debris. Ben Nevis may be the highest and mightiest mountain in the land but, from some angles, it is a soulless lump and many tourists rate their first glimpse of it as a major disappointment.

The Buachaille is a mountain for mountaineers and for the common man. It has the superstar image, a true rock legend.

It became a kind of talisman to me over the years. When anyone new wanted to join our climbing group and we were not sure of their ability, fitness or commitment, we always told them their first climb should be the Buachaille. It's not a hard day, so fitness should not be a problem, and if you do not fall in love with this mountain then there is no hope for you.

It has been a mountain of laughter and tears, of friendship and loss, champagne and birthday cake and whisky tributes to a lost friend. It has been a refuge when I feel down. There is nothing like a belt up the Buachaille in warm, wet conditions to blow away the stresses of that minor intrusion called life.

My first ascent was with Fergus. We were in Glen Coe for a September weekend. We were staying at the Kingshouse Hotel and planned to do both Buachailles the first day, the Ring of Steall in the Mamores the next, and finish with the Aonach Eagach on the Sunday. It was an ambitious programme but we were younger, fitter and clueless in those days.

Day one was a simple plan – up Coire na Tulaich and on to Stob Dearg, then back to the col and three miles along the ridge taking in the other three summits, before dropping off the end of Stob na Broige into Glen Etive and then starting up the short but relentless ridge to Buachaille Etive Beag.

The Munro book advice was to backtrack from Stob na Broige over Stob Coire Altruim and then drop down to the col between the Buachailles to save losing too much height. What did they know? Anyway, in those days we didn't do backtracks. It was forward or nothing. We would have made great Roman legionnaires.

Halfway up Coire na Tulaich we got chatting to a fellow walker. He had been touring Scotland for a couple of weeks and his mountain record was impressive. He was tall and thin, all gangles and angles, and his strange gait sometimes made it look as if he was walking in two directions at once. He wore thick, dark-framed glasses. His mannerisms were akin to Rowan Atkinson's Mr Bean but his nasally southern twang made him sound like Charles Hawtrey.

He kept finishing virtually every sentence with "but it's a laff, innit?" As in: "I nearly fell off that An Teallach last week but it's a laff, innit?" I could sense that we were not going to last very long as new mates.

After the initial interest was beginning to wear off, over to the right we spotted a stag, a magnificent beast, and this being rutting season he was in all his finery. He was also bold, not the slightest bit bothered by our presence.

I pointed out the stag to Mr Bean. He was not impressed.

"I don't like deer much. One of them wrecked my car the other day," he said.

I was going to ask why on earth he had a let a deer drive his car but, as will become apparent soon, I felt he might not appreciate my sense of humour.

Instead, I said: "He's safe up here. There is no shooting on this hill – a sign at the bottom of the road tells you that."

He looked at me strangely and there was silence for a few seconds. Then he said: "Are you saying the deer can read that sign?"

It was my turn for silence. Then I replied: "Oh yeah, there are a lot of smart deer up here, you know." He seemed satisfied. There was not a lot more said after that.

As we reached the head of the corrie for the push to the summit Fergus said to me quietly: "Let's run away now." We said our goodbyes and left Mr Bean to his fantasy world and the thought that he would be telling his friends in the south of England about the amazing deer of the Scottish Highlands that had learned to read.

Mad as it may seem now, we finished the circuit our way. It was a long, hard day and the old-timers in my office who knew the mountains could not believe we had done both Buachailles in this fashion.

From the little fort-like structure on the summit of the final peak, Stob na Broige, we dropped off down into Glen Etive. This is not a good idea and showed our naivety. It is covered in crags and slimy rock, a lot of it hidden under thick vegetation. I nearly came a cropper when I jumped down onto one ledge, half of it collapsing, causing one of my legs to sink into a rocky hole. The momentum threw me forward but my leg was trapped. I was lucky it didn't snap off. It took a long time to pick our way down the rest of the slope.

Once we hit the road we charged round to the path near Dalness, which gives a short, sharp ascent to Stob Dubh, the main summit of Buachaille Etive Beag, another perfect pyramid from this angle. We had lost a lot of unnecessary height and it was a constant uphill struggle to the huge cairn. We descended by the route in the Lairig Gartain that we should have taken up. It had turned into a mammoth expedition and we were in danger of missing our meal slot at the Kingshouse, so we found the strength to run back to the hotel as darkness descended.

Minestrone soup, mince and doughballs and jam roly-poly and custard. I can remember every bite to this day.

We did manage to do the Ring of Steall next day, five Munros (now four) from the head of Glen Nevis in another tough outing but by day three, with the cloud down, we felt we were too knackered to tackle the Aonach Eagach. You need clear heads for the most fearsome ridge on the mainland. It is one of the last places you want to feel your legs shaking.

In hindsight, it was a good decision not to tackle it with weary legs and weary hearts, clambering over wet rocks in zero visibility.

Glen Coe's notched ridge is a scrambler's heaven, a steep wall rising on the north side of the road which contains four peaks, two Munros and two tops. The main part of the ridge is a series of sharp pinnacles which provide a variety of problems and sometimes a lot of whimpering. It is very exposed in places and is not to be treated lightly. Not much chance of that, however, with its massive exposure and reputation for accidents.

The name Aonach Eagach, 'the notched ridge', is often whispered in reverential tones among the great walking unwashed. No problems for the rock tigers among us. But often the biggest problems are the queues to cross certain parts of the ridge – there is not enough room in places for overtaking.

With one car stashed at the Clachaig Hotel to avoid a long road walk at the end of the day, myself, Malcolm, Trev and Andy set off up the ever-steepening path which makes short work of the initial ascent and plants you on the ridge just short of the first summit, Am Bodach.

The first problem involves a climb down to the right and then a switch over through a gap on the left. I could see a long way down on both sides. It is the crux of the whole route in winter, when using a rope is the second wisest option after just not doing it.

The towering rock stack looks even more impressive 10 minutes later when you look back up at where you have been, but there are no more problems along the way to the Munro peak of Meall Dearg.

Now the notched ridge begins in earnest. There is a bit of a respite before the next real problem is encountered, a vertical chimney rising up from a gap which needs to be climbed to regain the main ridge. It was here that we found a piece of knotted, bloodied material hanging, suggesting a desperate bid to escape. We made a brief inspection of the area but there was no sign of anyone, so we decided to press on.

On another occasion a group of us were about to tackle this chimney when a dog, a Border Collie, suddenly appeared on the rocks behind us. The couple who had the dog stopped at this point to put him on a lead.

"How's the dog going to get up there?" we asked.

"No problem. He loves it. They're his favourite Munros."

We let them go ahead and the dog was off up the chimney, his natural crampons providing the purchase to rocket him up. Neither of us could decide if the wild look in the dog's eyes was down to over-excitement or just plain terror.

When you reach the top of the chimney, the bowl of the corrie behind often looks like it is on fire. Even in good conditions it is not unusual to see clouds frothing up from here in huge rolling banks, hiding the depths below.

With the bloodied sheet still in our minds, we climbed up to the next part of the ridge – and there was a tent with a pair of boots sticking out of the bottom. We stopped and called out but there was no response. Was this some poor person lying dead or badly injured after a fall? We had a feeling of dread as we approached the tent. No-one wanted to find a body. We took a moment or two to prepare for the worst. Trev finally got fed up of the waiting and pulled back the tent flap to reveal nothing but the pair of boots.

We discovered later that the day before, a walker travelling along the ridge had found someone lying injured at the foot of the chimney. He had fallen back down during his ascent and had a badly injured leg. The Samaritan had managed to knot together some of his and the guy's gear, got him up the chimney and then pitched his tent to make the casualty comfortable in the tent while he went for help.

The injured man was winched off by helicopter and taken to hospital but when the Good Samaritan asked where his tent was, he was told: "We don't rescue tents."

The Mountain Rescue guys had put his boots in place to look like there was someone in the tent. I am still not sure if that was meant as a joke to put the wind up unwitting walkers such as ourselves or a genuine attempt to make sure it stayed put. Either way, the climber's reward for helping the injured man was another trip to collect his tent. Just as well it's a great day out.

Another half-hour of scrambling up little gullies, squeezing through gaps on leaning towers of rock and edging your way along little ledges and we were at the final peak of Sgorr nam Fiannaidh. The view to The Ben to the north and down Loch Leven to the west are worth the admission money alone, but the excitement continues on the descent. Some people go all the way along to the notorious Clachaig Gully, a steep, loose descent on the edge of a deep cleft which has seen its share of casualties over the years, so much so that there is a sign advising walkers not to use this route.

We decided to descend a scree curtain, a constantly moving sheet of rock and shale on which it pays to keep moving as well. The combined noise of four people descending at the same time, plus the sliding and crashing of stones, rules out any chance of talking. For some reason I decided to look round at one point, only to see Trev scrambling to get out of the firing line and a dislodged boulder the size of a house brick hurtling towards my face at ever-gathering speed. I just managed to jerk my head to the side to feel the passing swish of the rock as it skimmed past me.

A neighbour once gave up scaling mountains for good after a similar narrow escape on the Buachaille's Curved Ridge. A slab tore loose from the grip of his partner above and scraped over the top of his head, leaving him bloodied and shaken. A dead hit would have sent him to his death. He reckoned he had used up his moment of good fortune and the next time he would not be so lucky. His optimism had all been used up.

Back in the early 1990s, the Cluanie Inn in Glen Shiel was a beacon for the mountain crowd. We spent many nights there and part of its unique charm was the husband and wife team who ran the place. She was the chef who provided the superb meals and he was mine host behind the bar, regaling his customers with tales of the hills. He was also in the local rescue team.

"Any word on the weather forecast for tomorrow?" I asked one night.

"Aye, it's gonna be a grand day."

"Any more details?"

"No, that's it. Gonna to be a grand day."

Thank you, Michael Fish.

Another night there was a discussion about reports of a possible ceasefire in the Balkans War. The barman had been chairing an impromptu debate and one of the patrons asked if there had been any breakthrough.

"Nah, they're a' fighting like buggery again."

Optimism and pessimism all in one wrapper.

Sometimes you are desperate to know what is going on but are sure it's probably better not to ask. Once, when I was heading back to the car on the Derry Lodge track after a long day in the Cairngorms, I met a huge guy coming the other way with a kayak on his back.

It was around 8pm and getting dark and this man must have weighed at least 18 stones. He said hello and asked me if I could confirm that he was going the right way. He didn't look as if he could walk very far, but he did look like he could have his kayak and eat it.

9
The White Stuff

WINTER WAS LATE IN getting a grip and so was I. The hills were showing only patchy snow but it was cold, wet and miserable nonetheless, that damp cold which seems to seep into your bones. The peaks I needed to do were far-flung. There were no journeys left now under three hours, and the thought of a long trip in the middle of the night and then a cold trudge with no possibility of any view was making it hard to get going.

My hill-going was restricted to some short days in Arrochar just to make sure the fitness did not slide. But the first good dump of snow and a few wild, storm-blasted days gave way to a spell of settled weather, and it was time to get back into action.

There is a dilemma at this time of year for the moonlight walker. If I travelled straight up from work at midnight, it meant arriving around 4am and the prospect then of either setting off in below-zero conditions in the dark or trying to sleep for a few hours in a freezing car.

If I headed home for a few hours' sleep before setting off, the chances of me getting up again to head off on a three-hour drive on a freezing night were slim.

I prefer to start walking as soon as I arrive, which is fine if it's a long walk in or there is a good path on the hill. But setting off up a pathless mountainside in darkness in winter is just asking for trouble.

The aim was to climb the three Munros near Spean Bridge. Beinn a'Chlachair, Geal Charn and Creag Pitridh are accessed from Luiblea, on the A86 in Glen Spean. Handily, there is a large parking layby just a few yards from the start of the access track. I arrived here about 3.30am and prepared with not much confidence to bed down for a few hours.

It does not take long after the car's engine has been switched off for the temperature to plummet. When it's -10 outside you are not many degrees better off inside.

I was wearing as much of my outdoor gear as possible – hat, gloves, thermals, fleeces, big jacket and I was inside my sleeping bag. Only my eyes and nose were not under cover.

But no matter how good your sleeping bag and hill gear, you always wake with a frozen nose and the feeling that you have been breathing in ice particles overnight. It does not set you up well for the day so, after just a couple of hours struggling to stay warm and with virtually no chance of getting any rest, it was on with the boots and out into the cold to warm up.

Although it was freezing and the overcast skies were providing no light, the track ahead was wide and clear, easily picked out with the head torch, and soon I was at the head of Lochan na h-Earba. Even in good sunny weather this long finger of water is a spot which radiates solitude. There is almost a reverential silence; the only sounds are the gentle lapping of the water, the wind caressing the sparse trees and an occasional plaintive cry of birdlife.

This is where the uphill work begins as the track degenerates into a path heading into the heart of the three Munros. The amount of snow was now slowing my progress, though. If it was deep here then how much deeper would it be on the hills? It was going to be hard going. I decided that discretion was the better part of valour, and that I would miss out Beinn a'Chlachair and concentrate on the other two. If I made good time then I could always change my mind on the way out. Besides, if I didn't do it this time, it was the nearest one to the road so it would not be a particularly long day when I returned.

It turned out to be a wise decision. By the time I was heading up the slopes of Geal Charn, I had slowed to a crawl. The cloud was thick and the wind and blowing snow ensured there was no visibility.

The path shown on the map was buried under feet of snow, but there was no view ahead anyway, so I stuck with a compass reading. I ended up contouring slightly to the left on to even deeper snow slopes, but a move to the right saw me pushing on and, after another half an hour or so of virtual blindness, I arrived at the large pile of ice-blasted rocks and the trig point which constitute the summit.

Geal Charn is another of Scotland's white hills, and it seemed a more than apt description on this occasion. It has an older, alternative name, Mullach Coire an Iubhair, 'the top of the corrie of the yew trees' but, like the trees themselves, it seems to exist no longer.

I was immensely pleased with myself. I had trusted my navigation on a day when I could barely see a few feet in front of me and was rewarded with a hard-won peak.

Creag Pitridh is a mere afterthought on this round, a tiny peak alongside its two big neighbours. Mutterings have been made in some quarters that it should not even be a Munro. I'm not in that club. It took a mere 15 minutes from the col to reach the top and by the time I had reached the summit the sky above was cloud-free. Below was an inversion layer, and all the peaks to the east were now poking up, their white caps shimmering in the sunshine. There was even a view over to Geal Charn, which was now showing me where I had been. Creag Pitridh may be small fry to some but, for me, it rescued the day brilliantly. Who says size matters?

The Geal Charn experience highlighted how far I had come in a short time. In the early days of our walking, Malcolm, Fergus and myself used to sit out the winter months, going into hibernation until spring broke through and the snows melted away. The winter mountains were for the real hard men, not amateurs like us. But now, not only was I a regular walker all year round in any conditions, I was happy and confident enough to go out in the middle of the night for snow walks, even when I could not see my hand in front of my face.

My winter skills training was mostly self-taught. Malcolm and I had decided we were ready to get out in the snow and move our mountain experience up a few notches. We had bought ice axes and crampons and we were going to put into practice in the winter terrain what we had been reading up on from the experts.

Because of the shorter daylight hours, Fergus had taken a pass on this new venture, but Malcolm and I could stretch the days a little longer because of a more flexible starting time at work.

After a practice run on Ben Lomond, where we were driven back by white-out conditions near the summit, we were on the slopes of Beinn Ime in the Arrochar Alps, doing winter training with our new toys. The added bonus for me was that it was a new Munro and, as Malcolm had already climbed it, I repaid the gesture a week later by going up Ben Vorlich again in freezing conditions to give him a new tick.

After reaching the summit with successful use of the spikes and axes, we found a good spot on descent to practise slipping and falling, building up the confidence and skills needed to arrest any slide. Malcolm had the added hazard of having to fight off his dog as he built up speed on the icy slopes, Scoop growling and trying to bite off his crampons, thinking them some kind of strange beast attacking the feet of his master.

Scoop was a real mountain hound, a Border Collie who loped along in lupine fashion with a look that said: "Don't mess with me." He didn't bother about any popularity contests. One time when we were in the Coire Cas car park at Cairn Gorm preparing for a climb we heard the oohing and aahing of tourists – before their tone changed rapidly to annoyance. They had been feeding the herd of reindeer that roam the plateau in this area and often come down to the car park for titbits, but now they were watching the deer charging up the hill, followed closely by Scoop. I turned to alert Malcolm but he was already off and running to try to collar Scoop. Nothing more for me to do. I sat and watched the spectacle of a man chasing a dog chasing a hundred or so deer, all getting smaller as they disappeared over the horizon. It was better than the cinema, a 3D chase sequence – and all for free.

Scoop was with us for most of our mountain days and, by the time Malcolm had sailed off for a new life in the USA, our four-legged friend had racked up more than 100 Munros.

Our winter of content taught us another valuable lesson on Ben Challum, a mountain near Crianlarich which normally entails a fairly benign walk up its southern slopes from the A82. In winter conditions, like most Scottish hills, it is a different beast altogether and twice I have been forced to call it a day, being battered into submission by the wind and accompanying blizzards.

Ben Challum is 'Malcolm's mountain', so it seemed to be a fine choice even with the blowing snow and heavily laden skies that greeted us when we emerged from the car in full winter gear. We walked through the farm and past the remains of St Fillan's Priory, where there are two ancient burial grounds. An old, disintegrating railway bridge gave careful access to the grassy slopes which were now rapidly disappearing under a white blanket. We were about a third of the way up the hill when the snow came on with a vengeance, driven fiercely into our faces by a bitter wind. The going became harder as the soft snow piled up, making crampons virtually irrelevant.

Every step was a struggle, but we reached the South Top of the mountain and crawled behind the cairn for some respite and to check our calculations for the final drive to the main summit.

We took our readings and set off north, but after a few hundred metres something strange happened – my compass was showing us heading in the opposite direction. It was impossible to be heard above the howling of the wind, so I tapped Malcolm on the shoulder and signalled him to huddle over.

"We're going the wrong way," I yelled, yet it came out as a whisper on the roaring wind.

"That's not possible," he said, but a quick check of his compass showed that we had appeared to have swung round 180 degrees.

All we could see in any direction was whiteness. There was a mountain out there somewhere, but now we had lost our bearings and recovering them was not going to be easy.

That was driven home even more emphatically when we took new readings. The compass had now swung back again, but we had no idea if that was because we had turned around and it was still pointing the right way.

Even Scoop had had enough. He looked the picture of misery, head down, ears down, a beaten-down hound. He was jumping up on Malcolm, whining, as if begging his master to get him the hell out of here. His paws had to be continually cleared of snow as it was freezing quickly between his toes making it difficult for him to walk.

Then it clicked – we had taken one set of readings while holding our ice axes beside the map. The metal had drawn the needle and thrown the compass into confusion. But we still did not know which reading was right and we had no idea as to where we were in relation to the ridge. We had to quit now and get off the mountain. The summit could wait, safety was paramount. But we still had to figure out which way was forward, which way was back.

There is a wisdom that says if you are caught in a whiteout, you can progress by throwing a snowball a few feet ahead and if you can see it land, you head to that point. You can then progress by repeating this process over and over. However, I believe it would take extreme bravery – or extreme desperation – to trust this method, and we were in neither position. Yet.

We had been standing still for a couple of minutes, like a pair of snowmen on the ridge, trying to work out what to do. I have often heard it said that a great calm can descend in moments of crisis, but had never experienced this sensation. However, as we stood there trying to make the vital decision as to which way to walk, the roaring wind was suddenly phased out of my hearing and all I could hear was silence, as if I had drifted into some kind of zen state (Malcolm said later that he had the same feeling). We were snapped out of our serenity seconds later when I spotted a faint figure passing not far from our left.

"Did you see that guy?" I asked. He had not.

"Someone just went past, heading down," I said. "I'm sure of it."

After a bit of deliberation, mainly through hand signals, and with no better plan, we turned to head in the same direction I thought I had seen the figure. Minutes later, with no sign of anyone, we arrived back at the cairn of the South Top. We had not been far away from our first reading and we had been on the right track after all. A moment's confusion had thrown us but, despite falling short of the peak, we came off the mountain with a feeling of self-satisfaction.

We had learned an important lesson. Never again would we take map readings with our ironmongery near the compass. More importantly, we had shown that we could follow one of the most important rules of mountaineering: know when to turn back. The hill will be there another day, the trick is to make sure that you will be as well.

Later that night in the pub we were regaling our narrow escape to our work colleagues when one of the ladies piped up: "God, that sounds so scary." And then, after a pause: "Do you find you get excited when you are in situations like that?"

"Excited is not really the word I'd use. It certainly gets the adrenaline flowing, though," Malcolm said.

"No, no, no, I mean *excited*. You know – down there. "

There was a stunned pause before Malcolm said: "What, you

think we're standing up there in driving snow and a minus 20 wind chill with a hard-on?"

"Well, it's quite a common thing with sportsmen and athletes."

"Listen, you could have the entire line-up from Hugh Hefner's mansion lying up there naked and you would not get excited."

I chipped in: "Plus, if you did, it might interfere with your compass readings. You know, like a radio mast. Anyway, the wee fella just snuggles away inside his big overcoat when it's that cold."

Maybe she had just become confused after reading a typo in a report of a mountain accident in one of the broadsheets a few months back. It reported that a couple had got into difficulties while on a hillwanking expedition. But I think we put her straight.

One week after the Challum debacle, Malcolm and I were again up to our knees in the white stuff, but this time there could not have been a bigger contrast. We were on Beinn Chabhair at Inverarnan in Glen Falloch, but we could have been somewhere in the high Alps.

The sky was a brilliant blue with not a cloud in sight, the sun was beating down and it was time to look cool and put on the shades. Now this was what the winter hills were all about.

Scoop had been doing his usual advance patrol and we had lost sight of him temporarily as we headed up on to more level ground beyond the tumbling waters of the Beinn Glas Burn. We spotted a few sheep and Malcolm became nervous (because of Scoop – not because he had worked in Aberdeen). He called the dog and after a few minutes Scoop came trotting back to us, looking a bit, dare I say, sheepish. We soon saw a possible reason why.

At the crossing of the ice-covered water, there were hoof prints leading to the edge. There was a break in the ice in the middle of the stream and, in the water under the hole, what looked like air bubbles breaking the surface.

They were coming up with ever-decreasing strength as if something were desperately trying to breathe underwater, and then they stopped. It looked like a sheep had gone through the ice, but there was nothing we could do, not without putting ourselves in the same danger.

I can't get a picture out of my head, of Scoop standing chuckling like Muttley as the sheep slipped away into the black, icy depths.

We were becoming experts in dealing with adverse weather conditions. A day traversing the three peaks of Beinn a'Bheithir was hampered by high winds and rain. The two-car solution came in handy, allowing us to start from the school in Ballachulish and finish a few miles further along in Gleann a'Chaolais.

Beinn a'Bheithir is either 'the hill of the monster' or 'the hill of the thunderbolt'. While the weather favoured the latter translation today, I prefer the former. From the road over the bridge at Ballachulish it certainly looks like a giant two-headed beast.

The monster was said to be a fearsome serpent which devoured anyone who happened to be passing. It was eventually killed by the wonderfully named Charles the Skipper, who lured it out to his ship with the promise of a feast. On the way there, it was impaled on a bed of spikes he had made from broken barrels.

The wind was blowing so fiercely uphill that our descent down a scree gully on the west ridge of Sgor Dhonuill became a lot easier and more carefree than it should have been. Malcolm and I ran down the loose ground with our arms out wide at times, being held back in our hang gliding by the constant upward wind. I hate to think what would have happened had it suddenly stopped. A much faster descent, no doubt.

The conditions were the same again when we tackled Ben Nevis and its adjoining Carn Mor Dearg arete. This time the biggest problem was the initial river crossing of the Allt a'Mhuilinn after we had cut over to Coire Leis from the lower slopes of Nevis.

The constant rain had turned the river into a torrent and we must have wasted at least half an hour looking for a place to cross safely. We eventually settled for a narrow section that could be crossed in two big steps – and a lot of praying – via a huge boulder in the middle of the rush.

Fergus went first and made it across to the other side. Malcolm followed to the rock where he stayed, wobbling, on his precarious perch as I held back the faithful Scoop. Then Malcolm said something I didn't take in at first.

"Right, pick the dog up and throw him to me," he said.

"What?"

"Pick him up and throw him to me. If he tries to cross by himself he'll get swept away."

"Are you completely mental?"

"Just do it."

"Okay, but he's not going to like it."

And that's how I suddenly became the dog hurling champion of Ben Nevis, picking up the unwitting Scoop by the collar and the back legs and flinging him into Malcolm's arms. Amazingly, he caught the dog and then threw him over to where Fergus was waiting.

There was one more surprise for us on that wet and miserable day. As we worked our way through the huge boulders that litter the ridge between Carn Mor Dearg and Ben Nevis, we stumbled across a soldier lying in camouflage in the rocks. Then another and another, until there was an entire ambush of troops.

"What are you guys doing here in this weather?" we asked.

"We're getting paid. What are *you* doing here in this weather?"

"Eh, having fun?"

Your 100th Munro should be a special one, so Malcolm and I were off to the Cairngorms seeking a break in the weather for once. We had climbed the highest mountain in Scotland two weeks before, therefore the ideal one for my century was the second highest, Ben Macdui. We were going to climb it from the ski centre car park taking in the peak of Cairn Gorm on the way.

The weather was superb on the drive up and we were raring to go but Cairn Gorm is notorious for having its own weather system. It started well, our walk up from Coire Cas taking place in calm conditions with a lovely autumn sun. Malcolm was calm as well, no reindeer herds in sight for Scoop to chase. When we hit the summit cairn the wind started picking up and the mist blew across in sheets until we were blanketed in a fine greyness with a shimmering light behind. No worries, the mountain optimist inside me said, it would soon blow away again. It did not.

The route over to Macdui is long and featureless with few landmarks to guide the way in thick conditions. In deep winter storms it can be deadly. We made it but it seems the change in weather had addled our brains and our co-ordination. We lined up for a picture with our fingers spelling out 100. I forever have the image in my photo album of Munro No.001.

It was while crunching our way back that Scoop decided to give us a scare. Scotland's own yeti, The Big Grey Man of Ben Macdui, is supposed to lumber about the plateau. When you are walking along in still conditions and thick mist, you can often hear footsteps crunching along behind you.

It is an eerie experience and has in the past spooked better men than us. In Victorian times, an Army captain was said to have been so unnerved by the feeling that something ominous was following him he emptied his revolver into the mist.

Now Scoop was standing, hackles up, growling into the mist behind us. We stopped but nothing appeared. The sound had stopped as well. As soon as we started walking again, the crunching began once more – and so did the growling. It took several minutes before he calmed down, although every so often he would glance back and growl a bit. No-one was devoured or shot and we arrived back at the car safely.

A return to the Mamores was next on the list, a chance to capture the views the books promised. Malcolm and I had gone up the night before to stay, planning for an early start the next morning. Not quite a nocturnal walk but I've had nights where there has been more light.

We set off at 7am, supremely hungover, so much so in fact that we had been walking for about an hour before we noticed that it had been raining all the way but, by this time, there was no point in putting on waterproofs. The damage had been done and, anyway, the light rain on our faces was pleasant and helped relieve the burning sensation in our heads.

We were heading for the outlying peak of Sgurr Eilde Mor and, just as we turned the corner into the beautiful Coire an Lochain, we saw a sheep sitting on the path. All the rest had scattered when they saw us coming, but not this one. It was holding its ground. Even Scoop was puzzled. He could not understand why it was not running away, and he was wary. As we moved closer, it became apparent that the reason it was sitting tight was because there was something wrong with its hind legs.

It was struggling to rise but finding it impossible to do so. We were unsure what to do. Even Scoop was circling around in confusion. We finally decided to leave the animal and try to find the farmer it belonged to on the way back.

We called in to the farm a few miles down the glen on our way back to let the farmer know about his injured sheep. He could not have cared less.

"Its legs are probably broken. You should have just finished it off with your ice axe," he said.

Now, picture the scene. The farmer, or one of his hands, comes round the corner looking for his flock and sees me standing over one of his animals, smashing its head in with an ice axe. No chance of that being misconstrued. At that moment, the only head we wanted to hit with an ice axe was his.

Almost a year later when I was walking that path again, there was the sheep's skeleton at the same spot. No-one had ever bothered to try to save it.

10
Dread Tired

THERE ARE TIMES WHEN you just know things are not right. That unsettling moment of doubt, a creeping dread which wriggles its way inside you to plant a big question mark in your head.

Often it is nothing more than a feeling that you are heading in the wrong direction despite what the compass and your own eyes are telling you. Other times it can be more sinister, a grumbling doubt that something malevolent is lying in wait, ready to pounce if you ignore the warning signs.

On such occasions, you must trust your instincts. I like to think that the amount of time I spend in the hills alone has heightened my senses, allowing me to develop an intuitive awareness of when all is well – or when something is not quite right.

The mountains can be intimidating, even on the finest days. Our country has a long and bloody history, and tales of lost spirits and mythical beasts abound. There is no shortage of ghost stories. Everyone who lives, works or plays in the wilds has an unsettling tale to tell. I have one or two myself but only once have I experienced a feeling of absolute dread, a feeling something so awful was about to happen that I turned my back on the mountains and headed for home without walking a single step.

Just a week after I had survived my fight with a tree in the middle of the night at the Mile Dorcha, I had left Glasgow around midnight filled with confidence for the long journey up the A9, then through Garve, Achnasheen and finally down Glen Carron. The two hills I was after were Moruisg and Sgurr nan Ceannaichean, a short and easy circuit of around five hours.

I had endured a bad day at the office, the result of a higher than usual series of nuisance phone calls from the Celtic and Rangers looney tunes brigade.

The worst nutters combed every newspaper and website every day looking for any perceived slight against their side.

There was always a conspiracy against one or the other, a grassy knoll in every opinion. Some nights you felt like weeping for the human race and other nights, like this one, I just got into my car and headed for the hills.

The weather forecast was good but this was not a route I fancied in pitch darkness. The way to the shapeless lump of Moruisg goes over pathless, boggy ground and I did not want to sink up to my waist in a swamp before I had really got going. I decided I would have a couple of hours' rest in the car, then head out when there was a semblance of light.

For once, I managed to drop off in the car, but it was not an untroubled rest. The chill was constantly prodding me, refusing to let me sleep. I was tossing and turning, trying to find the position to grab some sleep. Eventually I managed to drop off after a fashion. But I was not completely asleep, merely dozing. At one point, I heard the quiet pinging of light rain on the roof of the car.

Maybe it was the rising of the light that did it or maybe it was the gentle moaning of the wind. Maybe it was just my head dropping off the side of the head rest. But, suddenly, I shot bolt upright. I was

The summit cairn of Stob a' Choire Mheadhoin, complete with flag to celebrate my first moonwalk Munro, with the next target Stob Coire Easain behind

Malcolm tries to capture the moment the rising sun bursts out from behind
Ben Nevis from high on the slopes of Mullach nan Coirean

Taking a breather at the summit of Stob Ban in the Mamores
as the early-morning mist closes in to hide the sun

Scotland buried under a sea of cloud in this 5am view from Gleouraich, with Ben Nevis and the Aonachs on the horizon

Rolling clouds pour like a waterfall over the pass making Spidean Mialach
seem like a distant island, in this view from Gleouraich

Great view, shame about the breeks – Robert's red rubber trousers
dominate the landscape to Sgurr nan Conbhairean

Wisps of cloud blow away to reveal the Cairngorms peaks one by one as Robert and Evy near the summit of Mullach Clach a' Bhlair

An American on the Buachaille – Alex has a rest stop as cloud swirls around in the corrie below

Mullach na Dheiragain bathed in rays of golden sunlight at 4am as I look back over my route during the walk to Sgurr nan Ceathreamhnan.

Pheasants galore provide a welcome party during an early-morning winter jaunt up Geal Charn

Only the tops of the Cairngorms peaks are visible
above a sea of cloud from the traverse of Monadh Mor

Malcolm and the faithful Scoop, taking a
break from harassing sheep and policemen

Robert tries out his golf swing during a sensational early-morning
walk round Creag Meagaidh

Light in the darkness during a snowy descent
from Geal Charn

Early-winter sky tinged pink near Loch Arkaig at the start of the cold walk into the Sgurr na Ciche peaks

Celebrating the final Munro with Derek's sign on the summit of Am Faochagach

Fergus and I during the round of the Ben Alder peaks after an early start from Culra Bothy

Sky of many colours during an early-morning December ascent of Beinn a'Chochuill

Fergus shows his SAS skills during the crossing of the wire bridge at Steall in Glen Nevis

Fergus, possibly contemplating the profit margins on a caramel slice

The rising sun bursts from beneath the horizon to sweep across
the slopes of Beinn a'Ghlo

All the colours of the morning as early sunlight and shadow
highlight the peaks of Beinn a'Ghlo

startled. Something did not feel quite right. Something had really spooked me.

I shivered. It felt as if I was not alone in the car. I checked the back seat and then took a look around the vehicle. There was no-one else in sight, no cars on the road or parked nearby. The windscreen had a thin covering of frozen moisture. I looked down the glen. The road had a damp sheen. Sgurr nan Ceannaichean reared up through the front window. It had a dusting of snow on its flanks and the sky behind it was black, throwing threatening shadows over the slopes. It looked like a massive storm was rolling in ready to create havoc. Common sense told me this was unlikely but I still had a bad feeling, nothing specific, just the notion that it would be a bad idea to go up these hills today.

Had I had a nightmare? Or was I just exhausted and my mind playing tricks? I was certainly spooked but considering the number of times I had been out in the middle of the night, often in bad conditions, my foreboding just seemed silly.

I sat it out for a while to see if the weather prospects were going to improve. Nothing happened. The storm did not materialise, the snow did not start piling out of the sky, but that strange, disquieting feeling just would not go away. It was impossible to settle. I had a horrible feeling I had been given a warning which would be foolish to ignore. Something was giving me the opportunity to back away, and I figured I might not get a second chance.

It seemed crazy, but I had to trust my instincts. They had not been wrong before and now I had to rely on them. I decided to cut and run. I switched on the ignition and headed off on the long run back to Glasgow.

I was in my bed before midday. An eight-hour round trip to sleep in a car at the side of the road, and it had been all for nothing. But sometimes you have to go with your gut feeling. Knowing when to quit is a major attribute for mountain walkers and climbers. Even looking back on that night with a more composed eye, I have never regretted my decision to abandon the walk.

A few months and a few mountains later, I decided it was time to exorcise the demons which had driven me away from the two hills. This time there were no bad feelings, no nasty thoughts lurking in the back of my mind, just a determination to put this to bed once and for all. The music on the run up was upbeat. Shiny, happy people, no Thom Yorke wailing on about suicide or domestic violence.

My two peaks looked positively benign as I stood at the side of the car looking for bad omens in the sky. Bathed in the emerging, early-morning light they even looked welcoming.

Moruisg means 'big water' and while it may seem a strange name for a mountain, the amount of crap I had to wade through to get to the start of any climbing more than justified the title. In dry weather, it is wet. In wet weather, it is a massive swamp.

The name is thought to refer to the mountain resembling a huge wave breaking over the surrounding landscape. Moruisg does not live up to that romantic and flattering picture. It is not high on anyone's list of favourite hills and it certainly would not win a beauty contest. From the western approach, it is a big lump of a hill which drags you on upwards to the twin cairns at either end of the flat-topped, stony summit plateau. Do it from the other side and its corries offer a far more rewarding day, but the trek is much longer with a lot of backtracking.

It is also a hill that seems to draw in high winds. On another occasion while I sat at the summit with friends sheltering from the blasts, one of our party came rolling past head over heels, her somersaults aided by the fierce gusts.

But while Moruisg is the ugly sister, its neighbour on the other side of the scooped Coire Toll nam Bian, is definitely Cinderella. Sgurr nan Ceannaichean is a smaller but more shapely hill with hidden charms. There are two or three good options for ascent and the little tapered summit perch gives superb views of the surrounding peaks. There is also a great stalker's path which leads you down to the road in double-quick time.

Alas, Cinderella can no longer go to the ball. She has lost her place among the elite with a re-survey showing she is under the required height for a Munro but even if you are just a ticker, she's still worth climbing just to take away some of the pain of Moruisg.

Sgurr nan Ceannaichean is 'the peak of the merchants' or 'pedlars' and although there are no records to show who they were, in times gone by the main route from the east of the country to the west crossed this area and it may have been an important point of trade on the way.

The big surprise was meeting a family coming up this path. It was 8am and while the parents seemed delighted with their decision to go stravaiging from their camper van at this hour, the sullen daughter at the front hurrying away from mum and dad and the equally sullen son trailing behind, whacking every tree and bush with a stick, suggested that it had not been a unanimous decision. I suspect the parents will have paid dearly for this down the years.

It was an easy day and as I sat at the side of the road having breakfast, I stared back at the mountains and wondered what had freaked me out last time. Perhaps it was the thought of getting stuck with those kids for a day.

Given my aversion to sleeping in the car, I decided Gulvain would be a good bet for the next overnight trip. It lies hidden from passing motorists a few miles north up lonely Gleann Fionnlaighe, near Loch Eil on the A830 to Mallaig. The first hour-and-a-half of the walk is on a good track which meanders through mixed woodland by the side of the river and I figured that by the time I was at the foot of the hill my night vision would be good enough to start the steep walk up the grassy slopes.

Gulvain means the thrilling or filthy mountain but, for me, it is 'the hill of the heatwave'. Every time I have been up this behemoth it has been stifling. I've vowed that my next ascent will be in snow.

It is an unrelenting pull, a seemingly endless plod up a flight of grassy stairs and then, just when you think you have knocked it off, there is a sting in the tail – the 'real' summit is on the top of a huge pyramid even further on, with a dip between the pair which has to be re-climbed on the way back out.

Gulvain's scalp is not taken easily. You could be forgiven for believing that the reference to filth lies in the amount of cursing that must go on when walkers see their real target from this point, but it is more likely to refer to the huge, greasy dark slabs that cling to the steep faces on all sides of this hill. It is said that the slopes are so steep that stalkers were able to roll their slain deer down the sides, saving them the bother of carrying them out. Rolling down the hill has a certain appeal to the exhausted walker faced with a knee-breaking run down.

Gairich is a bold hill which soars up gracefully from the banks of Loch Quoich. It is a prominent landmark for travellers along the single-track road which runs for 22 miles from the A87 to the road end at Kinloch Hourn.

Gairich translates as 'the hill of roaring' or 'yelling' and refers to the noise the stags make on its slopes, as with so many hills in this area. You have to love a mountain called Roaring.

It is usually climbed from the Quoich Dam at the end of the loch, and there are some handy parking spaces there if you fancy a few zeds before heading up the hill. Just a little further on is a fabulous bivvy spot, a flat, gravelly area at the side of the road where you can sleep under the stars with the moonlit Gairich looming over the loch. It is one of my favourite spots and I invariably stop there, even during daylight hours, to take in the view.

I had travelled up under clear skies, the wonderful sight of the Hale-Bopp comet streaking across the heavens with a lightshow trailing in its wake keeping me company.

Glen Quoich is a deer-watcher's paradise. In the winter months following the rut, the road is lined with young stags exhausted and hungry with the massive weight loss incurred during the autumn mating battles. They are looking for food and on several occasions I have been approached by deer mooching for scraps. They are the street beggars of the West Highlands.

You cross the dam to pick up a very muddy path which leads across the shore, an expedition requiring you to pull your boots out of the ground on several occasions. A bit like walking in treacle.

Gairich is protected on all sides by cliffs and crags and the path provides one of the few routes through its defences. It is a rocky ascent but your hands will be called into action only a couple of times on the way to the roomy summit, and the views in every direction are superb.

Down to the left, the sunlit River Kingie looked like a silver snake slithering its way into a rocky refuge, while the views west along the ridge to the Rough Bounds of Knoydart promise many delights. It is always a temptation to the walker to carry on. However, I had a long drive back to civilisation and a deadline to hit so, sadly, I turned my back on a walk into the sunset and retraced my steps to the car.

A quick wave goodbye to all my deer friends and I was heading back into the madness of the sporting world.

With the exceptional spell of weather still holding, I was up Achnashellach way again. This time I was heading into Coire Lair, a massive corrie containing three majestic hills, two Munros and a Corbett. It is one of the classic circuits in the West Highlands.

The moon was full and providing enough light to get going right away and I gained height quickly on the twisting stalker's path which leads over rock rubble and polished slabs into the corrie. The view opens up magnificently when you reach this point, huge walls surrounding the walker on a grand scale.

To the left was Fuar Tholl, the smallest but probably finest peak of the three with its famous Mainreachen Buttress standing out in dark profile. On the right were the lighter, scree-covered peaks of Beinn Liath Mhor, the first target for today, and following on from that was Sgorr Ruadh, 'the red peak', its huge cliffs prominent on the left-hand side of the corrie.

As I branched off the path heading for Beinn Liath Mhor, the distant Fannichs range stood in stark contrast to their surroundings, like shadow puppets, the faint yellow glow of the rising sun backlighting them. Unfortunately that was as good as it got. As I rose on the steep path up the face of the first mountain the mist settled in and the further I climbed, the thicker it got. By the time I had reached the first cairn, visibility was down to a few yards. It was warm, but with no wind the prospects of a change in the conditions was not good.

The route along the pale scree ridge which give this mountain its name is a gentle roller-coaster but, with the mist down, there was an eerie silence broken only by the sound of the fragments of rock crunching under my feet.

The difference the weather makes on days like this is huge. Most walkers are prepared for whatever the elements throw at them but, if you set out in good weather and the forecast is off, it seems even more depressing. I don't mind walking in the rain, as long I know in advance it is likely to rain. Otherwise, it is as if you have been ambushed.

The lack of visibility had taken its toll psychologically and exaggerated the sheer weariness of walking at this time of night and I decided to abandon any attempt on Fuar Tholl. It would be a tired drive back to civilisation, but in terms of being let down badly by the weather, the next trip would trump that a hundred times over.

Evy was still mooning over her first overnight mountain trip in the Cairngorms so, hoping for more of the same, she and Robert left Glasgow after midnight to travel up to the Fannichs, where I would be waiting. The three hills on the menu were Meall a'Chrasgaidh, Sgurr nan Clach Geala and Sgurr nan Each.

We set off in brilliant early sunshine for what was supposed to be a cracker of a day. And it was a cracker – just not on the hills we were climbing.

Scotland was anticipating Mediterranean weather, but nobody had mentioned this to the Fannichs.

It started well enough as we followed the path down to the boathouse and then up the side of the lively waters of the Allt Breabaig. This can be a problem to cross in wet weather, or when it's threatening to be wet, or when someone just mentions the word wet, but we boulder-hopped it easily. Meall a'Chrasgaidh is not the biggest Munro. Its name reflects that – 'the hill of the crossing', just somewhere you pass over to get to the real hills. You take the direct route up through clinging grass and heather.

Now some of us have suspected for a time that Robert must be related to an ancient rain god. Either that or one of his ancestors performed rain dances for Scottish clans. Certainly he is around most times we end up with wet weather.

He has had summer holidays in Italy, Spain and Florida, where it has rained non-stop. Hillwalking weeks in Affric, Lochcarron and Corrour when it has sheeted down mercilessly.

And he lives in Glasgow, where they think about declaring a public holiday on any day it fails to rain. In ancient times, it was probably twinned with Atlantis, the natives falling to their knees in terror when that strange yellow ball of light appeared through the grey skies.

So predictably, as we moved higher up the ridge, the rain came on – and on – and on. By the time we had reached the twin cairns on the flat, exposed top we were soaked. This was not the plan. But the weather forecasters never get it wrong … so we were optimistic that the rain would clear away soon to give us our Costa sunshine.

We squelched our way across the corrie known as Am Biachdaich, 'the place of the fattening', a huge breakfast filled with lush grass where the deer come to feed in their thousands. And the rain became heavier. The ground here is usually wet but now it was like marshland. Our boots were sinking in the soft ground and the water was running over the tops of them. In such conditions it does not matter how waterproof your boots are; the water will always find a way in.

Rising steeply above us now was the beautiful Sgurr nan Clach Geala, 'the peak of the white stones'. Face-on, it looks like a giant sheet pegged to a high-level washing line. On a clear winter's day, when the snow is piled high and the sun is beating down, the sheet looks as if it has been laundered to a brilliant white.

As we made our way up the curving ridge through bands of rock, the rain turned to snow and the further we went up, the heavier and deeper it got. Near the summit it was knee-deep in places.

The path on to Sgurr nan Each was undetectable, as was the view in any direction. Geala's summit ridge is short and there are huge drops. Getting it wrong here could be disastrous, so we navigated down to the open slopes to our right and then worked our way back to the col, where it was pouring rain. The walk up the S-shaped linking ridge to Sgurr nan Each was now straightforward, if a tad damp, as we splashed through standing water and churned-up mud.

We did not even have the salvation of a pleasant walk out, but it was warm and sunny back at the car. A couple of miles down the road, it had been clear all day. The drive back was completed in blazing sunshine and, to add to Robert's annoyance, his wife told him she had been sunbathing in the garden all day. In Glasgow.

Standing under the cliffs of mighty Creag Meagaidh a week later, there could not have been a bigger contrast. The early sun was firing back glare from the huge rock walls, and the glass-like surface of the little loch was showing a mirror image of the Coire Ardair profile.

Robert and I had set off in the dark at 3am from the nature reserve car park, following the superb path through the remains of the ancient forest and into the ever-unfolding backdrop of the corrie. With the V-shape of the curious nick in the skyline known as The Window pulling us onwards, we were soon at the start of the day's ascent.

My last adventure had gone out the window here when my boots fell apart in the snow and I had to beat a hasty retreat, leaving Creag

Meagaidh for another time. Now there were only patches of snow in The Window and scattered over the bases of the cliffs, and the pull up the mountain behind the cliffs was straightforward. The view into this wilderness is almost primeval – it would be easy to imagine dinosaurs running around.

Creag Meagaidh is a mountaineer's paradise, its cliffs providing some of the finest winter climbing in Scotland. But it is also dangerous, prone to avalanche, and its massive summit plateau can be a navigational nightmare in poor conditions, with seemingly benign terrain suddenly leading to vertiginous drops cutting in on all sides.

It is a great reminder of the insignificance of man, a vast area with few landmarks. The main one is the massive Madman's Cairn, a 12-foot pile of stones and earth said to have been built by a man as a tribute to his deceased wife. In some books and maps it is referred to as Mad Meg's Cairn. Whichever name is used there is no doubt that it is enormous and someone was definitely mad. But even this huge pile shrinks into nothingness after a few steps away in this landscape.

The leftover snow on the edges of the slopes, still holding on during this June heatwave, provided a corridor across the short grass and stones to the summit. It was so stable that Robert ventured out on to one snowfield to practise his golf swing, his walking stick used like a three-iron, as he went for the Open championship at Cornicetie, his stance unaffected by the possibility of a collapsing cornice.

The long walk back down the ridge seemed to take forever, but that was principally because it was a photographer's dream. Creag Meagaidh is a mountain that is hard to leave behind.

11
The Longest Day

SKYE WAS ON THE HORIZON. The 12 Munros of the fearsome Black Cuillin are often the make-or-break peaks for budding Munroists and the trip at the end of June would probably decide if I was to complete my round.

I was now just seven short of the magic 200 mark and I planned to hit that target before tackling the most serious peaks in Scotland.

I had heard many tales of people getting so far round and then, for one reason or another, failing to finish. One man I had worked with, a real old-stager on the mountains, said he was going to use his early retirement to finish his round. He was sitting on 204 when he left the job, but he never did another Munro.

Others have done most of the hills "except for Skye". Another person I knew had racked up around 200 Munros before he went to tackle An Teallach – and then decided he had vertigo. Whether he did or not is up for debate; many people become spooked on An Teallach, and it has nothing to do with vertigo.

I had been casting envious eyes at the big glens west of Loch Ness.

A lot of the peaks in there are hard to get at and would normally take a few big expeditions to get round.

The chain of four Munros above Loch Mullardoch, for instance, involve a long, weary walk in for around three hours along a rough, lochside path, before you even tackle a hill. By the time you reach the first peak, An Socach, you have been going for at least five hours and there are three more huge mountains ahead. They are not easily won.

Affric is also a massive glen with peaks and ridges snaking out in all directions; attempting to do more than one or two hills at a time would involve a very long walk home.

In 1988, a fell runner named Jon Broxap managed to traverse 28 Munros in this area, a record for a 24-hour circuit. I was not in that league, but it seemed to me that the best way to tackle as many of these hills as possible in one outing was to devise a similar plan.

With the assistance of a friendly driver, I could start at the dam far up Glen Mullardoch, do the four peaks on this chain, drop down at the head of the loch, then start up another big ridge on the other side for three more peaks. Instead of a big walk out for two separate days, I could kill two birds with one stone by doing two big days in one go. It would be tiring, but it would save a return visit – and give me seven Munros to reach the magic 200.

First, I recruited my friend Jim to be the designated driver. Although he was not a serious mountain walker, he loved the outdoors and the prospect of touring, so he jumped at the idea of this adventure. He was happy to take me to the village of Cannich, about 10 miles west of Loch Ness, then on to the Mullardoch Dam, where we would part company. Jim's journey would take him round to Glen Cluanie, where he would stay the night at a local hostelry before picking me up 24 hours later.

Meanwhile, I would charge across the Mullardoch hills, then drop down to start up Mullach na Dheiragain, over to the massive Sgurr nan Ceathreamhnan and then An Socach (another one) before heading down to the remote hostel at Alltbeithe in Glen Affric, from where I would walk out to our meeting spot on the A87 near the Cluanie Inn.

When you describe the expedition like that, it sounds easy, but these were huge, remote hills and, once in the heartland, there was no turning back, no easy opt-out.

Since it was summer and the forecast was good, I ruled out any thought of taking a tent. I wanted to travel light and, rather optimistically it seems now, intended to keep walking the whole time, with just a 10-minute rest here and there.

I did have a survival bag, a bright-orange, heavy-duty plastic effort which I kept in my rucksack for emergencies. It had never been used in anger, but I could crawl into it if I needed to sleep. It was my second survival bag, the first having worn out years ago after use as a sledge to descend snow-plastered slopes. Well, it was faster than walking. You could build up a fair speed on it, necessitating the use of an ice axe for a brake. I had been fortunate enough never to have to use it in a life-or-death situation.

It was the same story with food. Rather than burden myself with the extra weight of stoves, plates, cutlery and cups, I would rely on snacks such as power bars and nuts and raisins.

I don't eat much on the hills. As long as I have plenty of fluid – water purification tablets are a godsend – and a big plate of porridge before setting off, then all's well.

I know members of the Mountain Rescue Team who carry only a couple of Mars bars in their packs for emergencies, while other people load up with what looks like a family picnic for a day's walk.

One of my regular walking mates, Crawford, has an appetite like a horse and almost needs a second rucksack to carry all his food and drink. On one memorable winter's day in the Cairngorms, he ate eight mini-pork pies at one stop along with a sandwich and some sweets. His partner, Rebecca, was not far behind him. Our very own Nosh 'n Becks scoff their way round the mountains. A typical trip to Glen Coe, for instance, involves a stop in Tyndrum for an all-you-can-eat breakfast before stocking up with sandwiches and pork pies to beef up their luncheon box for the hills, and then often a snack back at the car or on the way home. It's like a day out with locusts.

Fergus, meanwhile, took the prize for the most elaborate sandwiches. One particular concoction consisted of coronation chicken and beetroot. He was also a fan of cold baked beans. Strangely, he never moved on to a caramel shortcake sandwich.

Then there is Carol. She always upstages everyone else with her dainty sushi box containing a variety of dishes in their own compartments. She would not look out of place on the summit of Mount Fuji. On one occasion, she even brought her own home-made pakora. Sitting alongside that lot, I always look pathetic with a fruit-flavoured shoelace or handful of wine gums.

So, with my rucksack stripped to the bare minimum, I was deposited at the dam at 11 o'clock on a beautiful morning after a leisurely drive over from the east coast. The sun was shining, the reflection bouncing off my new boots. I felt in good spirits, but Jim looked worried.

"Are you sure you'll be fine? It just seems a hell of a long way. No, actually, it *is* a hell of a long way."

"It'll be fine. I've got everything I need."

"I suppose. Gene Pitney was only 24 hours from Tulsa and that was a hell of a lot further away. Of course, he was in a car and he did have a woman waiting for him with open arms."

"That's a really bad example. Gene didn't make it. He was on his way to Tulsa, but then saw a welcoming light and stopped to rest for the night. And then he met that other bird."

Jim just looked stunned.

He walked with me up part of the path along the loch side, then waved farewell and I was on my own, heading north towards the twin rounded mounds of the first peak of the day: Carn nan Gobhar. It did not take long for the first small problem to arise. My new boots, although they had been broken in, were still stiff. By the time

I hit the first summit just two-and-a-half hours after setting off, I had blisters. The flat, stony summit can catch the unprepared walker out in thick weather. The first cairn on the ridge is substantial, but it is not the summit marker. That lies across a small hollow a few hundred metres further on.

Carn nan Gobhar is 'the hill of the goats', but you'll be lucky to see any up here these days. In times gone by they were hunted for their meat and skins. However, there is a tribe of long-haired, wild goats which roam along the shores of Loch Mullardoch. Even if you don't see them, you will likely catch a whiff of their musky scent.

I was certainly hobbling along like an old goat. But, after a few minutes of foot repair, it was on to Munro No.2, Sgurr na Lapaich, 'the peak of the bog'. It towers above Carn nan Gobhar and is a 1,000-foot push up an ever-narrowing spur with mighty corries on either side and the crag-bound Loch Tuill Bhearnach sitting down on the left, but I was making good time and the blister problem seemed to have receded.

Sgurr na Lapaich is the highest peak on the ridge and from there the views are expansive. I could pick out every peak I was hoping to conquer and was developing a true feel for the distance and climb involved.

The top is marked by a huge circular cairn with a trig point in the centre on to which someone has scratched the name Petra. Who knows how long that particular piece of graffiti has been there and who it refers to?

The mountains are littered with names and memorials for lost friends. Some are subtle, some jar the sensibilities. While the sentiments may be right, the result can sometimes amount to nothing more than a trashing of our wild places.

The summit of Ben Nevis is already a huge rubbish tip which needs a tidy every so often. The iconic Buachaille Etive Mor in Glen Coe is another popular spot for memorials and the scattering of ashes. A party of us make the ascent of this hill every year in early

July to remember our good friend Trevor, who died there in 2004.

Trevor was a force of nature, a mini whirlwind who lived life to the full. We had been planning a walk up the Buachaille on the Saturday to celebrate my 50th birthday. In typical Trevor fashion, he thought it would be a great idea to have a bottle of champagne and a card waiting at the summit when we arrived. But this would mean someone climbing the mountain the night before. He set off alone sometime after midnight on Thursday. It was only later on the Friday, when he hadn't appeared for work and no one could contact him, we began to suspect something was wrong.

Later that day his car was found in Glen Coe, and then came the devastating news that mountain rescuers had found a body. We'll never know exactly what happened, but the theory was that he been climbing Curved Ridge, a more serious route than the normal walking ascent, and then, accidentally or deliberately, had strayed on to the even more serious Crowberry Ridge. Trevor was a superb climber and had always been talking about going up Curved Ridge. It was well within his capabilities, even without a rope. Crowberry Ridge, however, was not. We reckoned we could picture him thinking it was too easy and then deciding to take on a bigger challenge.

Trevor's ashes were scattered in the stream that flows down into the Coire na Tulaich. We always stop to pour a dram into the water on our annual pilgrimage. His parents lay some flowers on the bridge approaching the mountain every year.

One year, while on the main summit, Stob Dearg, we saw a triangle of ashes, a mini-mountain which hadn't been scattered to the winds but just dumped in one large pile. No doubt they blew away soon, but I'm sure it wasn't quite how the deceased would have planned it.

I continually emphasise to my family how I want my remains scattered at the top of the Buachaille, with the threat that if they try to sell me short they are cut out of the will. I do not wish to be a pyramid of dust, dumped haphazardly.

One of the most poignant memorials is on the approach to the Conbhairean hills in Glen Shiel, where the message on a rock is for a 16-year-old boy "lost in these hills" back in the 1960s. The teenager would now be a pensioner and the people who arranged the inscription are likely long gone, but his memory will live on forever in that lonely spot.

I was now heading down south-west to the pass, the Bealach Toll an Lochain, with its twin bodies of water glistening like jewels far down in the corrie to my right. This is an incredibly beautiful spot, with views over to the Monar peaks and soaring ridges on all sides, and the steep pull up to the long high-level ridge of An Riabhachan, another massive mountain, is well compensated.

As I reached the first of the chain of four summits on the hill, the sky ahead appeared ominous. The predicted dry day was being overpowered by towering black clouds as the wind started to pick up. Within minutes, the rain was thundering down and my waterproofs were having to work for a living. It was over quickly, but steam was rising from my clothes and I had the disconcerting feeling that I would not be dry again on this walk.

From the final summit of An Riabhachan, the ridge turns west again and becomes rocky, sharp and narrow. In full winter conditions it could be a serious proposition, but apart from a bit of hands-on at times, there was no problem and I was at the summit trig post of An Socach by 6.15pm, seven hours after setting off. So far, so good.

However, as I descended to the head of Loch Mullardoch, the heavens opened again and the water was running over my boots as I squelched down to the river. The irony was that although there was water everywhere, I had not drunk any for a couple of hours.

I had met no-one and my only companion was a huge rainbow which followed me alongside the stream in Coire Lungard to the low point of the round.

The head of Loch Mullardoch is truly remote. Further to the east there is the Seldom Inn, a small estate hut, locked to hillwalkers but used by stalkers and estate workers. The mountains ahead of me were starting to grow in size. It would be some pull up the next one, but I had to keep going to stay on target. It was 8pm by the time I reached the river crossing, and the evening sun bathed the hillsides ahead of me in a golden hue.

Despite the heavy rain, I traversed the Gobh-alltan without a hitch and commenced my leg-heavy plod up to the next Munro, Mullach na Dheiragain.

The immediate difficulty facing me was that I had given away a massive height advantage. From being at nearly 4,000 feet at one point, I was back down to about 800 feet and facing a re-climb of about 3,000 feet, with ups and downs over other tops, to reach Munro No.5. It was exhausting, both physically and psychologically, and I was having to bully myself into believing I could keep going.

After two hours of consistently slower going, I was only a few hundred feet from the ridge, but my body had had enough. I could not put one foot in front of the other. I had to have a rest. I looked around for a good sleeping spot, then sat down for a bite to eat. The sun was going down, the brilliance of the light akin to a far-off nuclear explosion, its dying embers making some of the peaks seem as if they were on fire.

I had eaten some fruit and crisps along the way, but the power bars were a mistake. When you are as dehydrated as I was, the last thing you need to consume is something with the consistency and taste of reconstituted cardboard and woodchips. Chewing became harder than walking. I seemed to be burning up more calories than I was taking in.

Everything I wore felt damp, but exhaustion was taking over so all I could do was crawl into my bivvy bag. My rucksack was my pillow and I sealed the top of the bag and settled down to try to sleep.

I am sure that if you were freezing to death somewhere and needed emergency shelter, these bags could be a lifesaver. But when you are wet and it is reasonably warm outside, they are an unmitigated disaster.

As I lay in my bag on the side of the hill, the condensation inside became unbearable. I was wetter in here than I had been out in the rain. Meanwhile, the wind had picked up and I was being buffeted from side to side. I felt like a fairground goldfish in its plastic bag, which had been pitched into a heavy sea. I was drowning. I could just see the newspaper headlines:

HILLWALKER FOUND DROWNED IN PLASTIC BAG.

After a couple of hours of no sleep and a constant steam bath, I decided enough was enough. Storm or no storm, I had to break free. I pushed my way out of the bag to emerge like a drowning man coming up for air. Within seconds I had dried out. The wind I had felt battering me was actually a gentle breeze, pleasantly warm, and the relief when it washed over me was immense.

It was dark, but the lift I experienced from being dried out convinced me to get moving. A quick change of socks and I was heading up to my next target.

It took only about an hour to climb to the summit of Mullach na Dheiragain and it was 2.45am when my head torch picked out the cairn. The blood-red sky in the background to the north gave me a frame to take a picture of what was, essentially, a pile of rocks in the darkness. The route onward is long but fairly easy and I had a spring in my step again as I headed south, then south-west, on the curvature.

Looming ahead next was the monster of the trek, the tongue-twisting Sgurr nan Ceathreamhnan. It sits like a giant squid in the centre of this mountainous region, tentacles reaching out in all directions, sucking in several subsidiary peaks along each arm. 'The peak of the quarters' is well-named, its long, distinct ridges dividing the land neatly into parcels.

As I approached the climb to the summit, the morning glow turned the whole mountain red, as if Dante himself had decided to take a hand in its appearance. The view back to Dheiragain was no less spectacular, the far peaks bleached out while the ridge behind me stayed in the shadows, just wisps of white where the early cotton-wool mist rose like steam off the land, a spectacular light show being played out for an audience of one.

The massive pile of rocks at the summit of Ceathreamhnan provides an uncluttered view in every direction. A hop and skip along is the west top, a rocky mound that lords it over Gleann Gaorsaic but, tempting as it was, I was done with hopping and skipping for the day.

Now it was all downhill, so to speak. The east ridge of Ceathreamhnan goes over two other peaks before depositing you at the col, where the ascent of the final Munro of the round awaited. Another An Socach, but this time a smaller one, almost an afterthought among these giants.

By the time I reached the point where I should start climbing, it did not appear so insignificant. It looked like the biggest hill I had encountered so far. It was almost 7am and I was starting to feel exhausted again.

Physically I was at a low point but, more significantly, I was mentally shattered. The thought of climbing another hill was almost too much to contemplate. The path down to the hostel and the way home was beckoning. And a pint. And something to eat that did not taste of cardboard. And even the welcoming arms of Jim.

However, after a serious debate with myself, I bit the bullet – it was tastier than the power bar – and started the ascent to the summit of An Socach. It took less than half an hour. I had overcome exhaustion to complete my task: seven Munros with just a two-hour waterlogged rest for a non-sleep. There were three-and-a-half hours left to reach my rendezvous with Jim.

The first part down to the lonely and seemingly deserted youth hostel in Glen Affric was easy enough on a decent path, but the final five-mile leg over the pass An Caorunn Mor meant a slight re-climb which, at this stage, was the last thing I needed.

It was a struggle and I was running late but, by 11.45am, just 45 minutes over time, I reached the end of the pass to see Jim waiting at the parking place. Then I collapsed. My body decided it had done its job. Having taken me round 15 peaks over 24 hours, it was now going on strike.

Jim gave me a hand to the car. He had seen me striding down the glen and thought I looked in great shape and was surprised when I keeled over.

After a few minutes' recuperation, I was able to tell him I needed to go to the pub. One pint of lager, a gallon of water and a bowl of soup later, we set off down the road ... so I could start work at 5pm.

I never made it. I fell asleep in the front seat and, when we reached my flat in Glasgow, I had to be helped to bed, a shivering wreck. My call into work was garbled and the rumour spread that I had suffered a bad accident on the hills.

I had once been described by a colleague on the news desk as a future lead brief, a two-paragraph piece with a head picture that covered fatalities. The familiar cry when I left the office to set off on another trek was: "Have you remembered to leave an up-to-date picture of yourself. Just in case?"

Okay, I was suffering from exhaustion, had blisters, and my back, sides and nether regions were badly chafed. But, apart from a near drowning in a plastic bag, the experience was not that bad.

Eighteen days later, Fergus and I were off to Skye. With my 200th Munro notched in such trying circumstances, the Misty Isle's finest were a dawdle in comparison. We spent a week there and managed not only to finish the 12 required peaks in the Black Cuillin, but also took a detour to climb the magnificent and stand-alone 'hill of screes', Beinn Sgritheall, round the coast at Arnisdale, before heading home. It was time for a holiday.

12
Your Number's Up

THE MUNRO LIST IS an ever-changing feast. When Sir Hugh Munro published his Tables of Heights over 3,000 feet, in 1891, the contents demolished the belief that there were only about 30 peaks of that height in Scotland. He estimated there were up to 10 times as many, and set out to climb them all.

He divided his peaks into 283 mountains and 255 subsidiary peaks, or Tops, a grand total of 538. The list has always been open to interpretation as to what constitutes a Munro and what makes it a separate mountain and, every so often, it is tinkered with by the mountaineering authorities, often because of modern mapping methods.

The man who let the Munro genie out of the bottle never managed to complete his own list before his death in 1918, at the age of 63. He failed in a few attempts to conquer the Inaccessible Pinnacle in Skye and had never climbed Carn Clioch-mhuilinn in the Cairngorms, which he had saved for his last peak (it was later demoted to a top).

His accounts of wild treks across the toughest terrain in search of peaks, sometimes lasting days, make the modern hillwalker feel humble. He did have his chaffeur waiting for him with a mug of hot chocolate and dry clothes, whereas the likes of you or I would have to settle for a packet of chocolate buttons at best, but his expeditions were still epic.

The honour of being the first Munroist fell to the Reverend A.E. Robertson in 1901 – although it was thought he never actually climbed the Inn Pinn, either, which was still regarded as a Top – and it would be 22 years later before the full round was conquered again.

By 1960, the number of people who had conquered the list had risen to 42 and, by 1970, it had hit 100. The new craze was snowballing. Nowadays, about 200 people every year complete the Munros. When I completed in 2000, I was No.2433. More people have done the Munros in the last 11 years than between 1901 and 2000, and the number is fast approaching 6,000.

By 1981 the target for would-be Munroists was 277, but in 1997 that figure was revised upwards again, with eight mountains promoted and one struck off, taking the new tally to 284. And just to show that the list never stands still, Sgurr nan Ceannaichean was recently booted out for lying about its height, with the hard-to-get-at Beinn a'Chlaidheimh following soon after. Both were victims of satellite mapping, which showed they were lower than the magic 3,000-feet mark.

The changes in 1997 were a good example of how going for Munros alone is a fool's game. Every one of the promoted mountains was already a prominent peak and part of a ridge that most mountain lovers would climb anyway. How many people go up Buachaille Etive Mor in Glen Coe, for example, and just go to the main summit, Stob Dearg? Most continue along the ridge, making a day of it, strolling over two further Tops before reaching the promoted Munro at the end of the ridge, Stob na Broige.

Anyone who takes the shortcuts for a quick tick deserves to have to go back up to complete the entire ridge for their prize. I have no sympathy. I would have relished being in the company of someone who had just done the Munro peaks in this fashion when they heard the news.

There are always rumours about other peaks which could be moved up at some stage. Conquering them all is the only way to be sure. Whatever the tally, if you complete the list at that point then you are a Munroist.

Non-climbers do not understand the game. When the changes were announced in the autumn of 1997, I lost count of the times I was told by a smiling face: "Well, I guess that's a few more you have to go out and do then."

My equally smug reply was always the same: "Actually, I've already done them."

The response always brought a puzzled look – why would you climb hills you didn't have to?

Another example of how non-hill goers simply don't get it came when I was watching the film *Cliffhanger* with my wife. The film is nonsense – you can watch it with your brain switched off. It appealed to me, though, because it had been filmed in the Dolomites and the mountain scenes were breathtaking. The downside was that it features Sylvester Stallone as a mountain guide trying to thwart a gang of criminals chasing lost money in the snow-covered mountains.

At times Stallone hangs from a fingernail while being shot at by men with automatic weapons and people hurling explosives at him. He even has a fight on board a helicopter, dangling over a cliff.

At one point, as Stallone clung on to his partner by his fingertips over a huge drop, Alison turned to me and said in all seriousness: "That's not what you do, is it?"

"It's very similar," I said. "There's just not usually so many people shooting at me."

If you get hooked on mountains, then you want to climb everything. Granted, there are some you ascend and then hope you never see again, but they are few and far between. The Munros are only a start. There are many great hills out there, and size is not everything.

Unlike Sir Hugh, I had managed to climb the Inn Pinn during our sweep of the Black Cuillin. But that had been more than a month ago, and I was now back from a break in Florida feeling refreshed and ready to go again. I also needed my night-time fix, so I decided to head for Aviemore to tackle Bynack More, one of the outliers in the northern Cairngorms.

The Cairngorm hills are ideal for night walking. They feature long walk-ins on superb paths which give you a few hours' easy walking before dawn breaks and the proper climb begins. By the time I arrived at Glenmore Lodge it was 3am and, with clear skies, there was no need for a torch.

It was breezy but warm, the collective sighs of the trees on either side of the track a constant background whisper as I made my way into the darkness. There were a few scattered tents sited round the ruins of the dilapidated Bynack Stables, but no sign of life as I passed on the wide ribbon of soft gravel that cuts straight uphill to deposit you on an open plain. Within an hour it was light and, despite the strong wind trying its best to push me back, I was at the pale, red pancake stacks of the summit by 6am.

The mountain's name comes from the pointed top, unusual for a hill in this range, that resembles the shawl or coif, headgear once worn by the women of this region to indicate they were married. Ahead lie the Little Barns, a series of granite towers piled up and coloured like chunks of kebab meat on skewers, a worthy diversion if you have the time, before the ridge swings round to the south-west towards Loch Avon and Cairn Gorm.

Bynack More is one of the easiest Munros, a gradual ascent gaining height gently and a good enough path to run down on the way out. On the way back, I took a look in at the bothy where two half-dressed young Dutch women were having breakfast. They asked if I'd like some. I had to pass – it was food after all and I don't do food at that time of day. Well, I assume it was food they were offering.

It is unusual to escape the wind entirely on the hills in Scotland. Even on the calmest of days down below, it can be blasting the skin off your face further up. Sometimes a breeze can be a blessing, especially on hot nights like that on Bynack More, but a week after that trip I was to witness a perfect storm in miniature.

I had left my transport at the wooded car park in Craig, near Achnashellach, around 3.30am and was heading south on the track which leads into the heart of the Glen Carron mountains.

The dark was rising and there was no need for a torch as I walked in accompanied by just the rushing of the wind through the trees and the occasional high-pitched screech or scream of small birds and animals slaughtering one another.

Sgurr Choinnich and Sgurr a'Chaorachain are jammed tightly up against one another and are a natural grouping to tackle. There were tents pitched on the banks of the Allt a'Chonais, but no sign of any life as I headed up to the opening obstacle of the day, a wire bridge across the river.

I came first to a wooden bridge, but there was a sign politely requesting walkers not to use this one, but to head for the wire bridge further on. Good one, guys. I'm sure there are estate workers hidden somewhere in the long grass nearby with a telephoto lens having a laugh at some of the attempts to cross.

The 'bridge' comprises two taut wires, one about a foot above the water and the other at chest height. There is a wooden spar running parallel with the bottom wire and you edge your feet along this while holding on to the top wire. By the time you reach the middle of the crossing, your weight has forced the wires down towards the water so that it feels as if you are suspended face first, belly down over the water. Just as you feel you are going to be tipped in for an impromptu soaking, the next movement sees the wires rising again, gradually, until you reach the other side. It is easier to wade across the water.

A good stalker's path now wends its way south-west to the Bealach Bhearnais, 'the pass of the sauce' (not really), and the foot of Sgurr Choinnich's west ridge. The weather so far had been calm, overcast but with high cloud and decent visibility, but about halfway up this ridge I could feel a change. The wind was picking up from the south and, as I looked in that direction, I could see thick, black clouds travelling up the glen at a rate of knots.

Within seconds I was being buffeted by a ferocious wind, and was almost knocked off my feet. I was struggling to walk. It felt like I was being pummelled by Mike Tyson and every blow was getting stronger. I crawled behind a rocky outcrop to shelter from the wind and to get my breath back. I could hear the wind thumping against the rocks.

Then, within a couple of minutes, almost as fast as the mini-hurricane had arrived, the howling had stopped and it was calm again. This was a truly bizarre episode.

Everyone has experienced localised weather at some time, whereby you can stand in gorgeous sunshine watching the rain fall just a few hundred metres away, but I had never been caught in a wind that seemed to target an individual.

The continuing route up the rocky west ridge was conducted in an almost unworldly calm, and I kept glancing nervously over my shoulder, waiting for the wee slugger to make a second assault.

From the cairn on the short, narrow summit platform of Sgurr Choinnich, the rather misleadingly named 'mossy peak', there was no sign of any further disturbance, just a clear view of where I wanted to go next.

A short push down, and then up, took me on to Sgurr a'Chaorachain in just over half an hour. Chaorachain is 'the peak of the little field of berries', but there are no rowan trees or berry fields. It is a bold, strong peak which commands the high ground with superb views, but its crowning glory is the subsidiary Top of Bidein an Eoin Dearg, further along its spur. Some believe it is only a matter of time before this is classed as a separate Munro, so it is worth taking the extra 30 minutes or so to climb to its soaring peak.

The route down from here is crag-rimmed, so I returned along the ridge and then charged down the steep but easy shoulder of the grassy north-east spur. I dropped height rapidly and was soon back on the inward route. And there was not one more breath of wind.

By early September 1997 my sports workload had taken a bit of a back seat for once. News was king. The death of Princess Diana in Paris a week earlier was still occupying the bulk of the paper and we Scots were on the verge of voting yes to having our own parliament for the first time in nearly 300 years.

It seemed rather apt that I would be out wandering the hills under cover of darkness like that forerunner of Scottish independence, Bonnie Prince Charlie. It is a consequence of solo walking that your mind tends to wander. The drive to my destination usually gives me the time to digest the day's work and problems and, by the time I am out in the fresh air with a pack on my back, my mind is clear and relaxed. If I have nothing serious left to think about, the inner debates tend to be more surreal.

Tonight it was old Charlie's turn. The vertically challenged, no-very-bonnie, French/Italian scallywag seemed to spend much of his time dodging about the mountains in the middle of the night. Don't know how many Munros he did, but the total cannot possibly have topped the number of caves he is supposed to have been in.

Just about every area of the north and West Highlands has a Prince Charlie's Cave marked on the map. He probably had some overseas as well. He was a man of caves, the major property magnate of the mid-1700s, but you get the feeling if he was around today he would either be a penniless pest, hanging about on street corners scrounging for money, or a contestant in the Big Brother house.

Going up Nevis Gorge in the dark is always inspiring. The path weaves its way from the car park at the head of the glen and, as

I climbed higher into the gap, I felt the steep rock walls of lower Ben Nevis, with trees clinging on for dear life, while hundreds of feet below I heard the thundering of the Water of Nevis. As the destination neared, I made out the shapes of boulders, some the size of houses, providing a series of obstacles for the torrent to bubble and boil over and around.

In less than half an hour I emerged into peaceful, grassy flats with the impressive Falls of Steall as a backdrop. A three-wire bridge carries you over the river into the Mamores. There are often many tourists hanging around in the long summer days, wary of taking a chance on the wires, but anxious to see others have a go.

Fergus and I once crossed over, watched by a capacity crowd. When we reached the other side, a couple of people applauded and one asked if we were in the SAS. If we had been, we would probably have killed them for being so annoying.

I wasn't going for the crossing this time. Instead, I was taking the path further up, past the old ruin of Steall, and then cutting up on to Sgurr Choinnich Mor, a huge outlying hill of the Grey Corries.

The dawn was having a longer lie-in with each passing day so the head torch was on until I started the climb up to the ridge. When the light finally started to rise, it was not the glorious sunshine I had hoped for. Instead, the mountains looked like they were being caressed by a thin sheet of grey gossamer which seemed to bounce gently up and down on the summits. There was not a breath of wind and the view from the summit was decent despite the greyness that was clinging on doggedly, all around.

The best part of the day was on its way. By the time I had reached the path to head back to the car, the sun made a sudden and blistering appearance. It was still mid-morning and I had a few hours to spare – I knew the perfect spot to enjoy the rays.

Right in the centre of Nevis Gorge there is a huge boulder which is shaped like a giant armchair. There were no towels laid out on it so, after a short, careful scramble from the path over the adjoining rocks, I was lying in a suntrap with the water careering down either side of my perch.

By this time the foot traffic was getting heavy and there was no shortage of surprised looks from passing walkers as they spotted yours truly lying in the middle of the river in the gorge. The only prop missing was someone to bring me a cocktail.

Unfortunately the weather had started to turn and, although it stayed dry, there was no early lifting of the curtain of cloud, and there was a dampness in the air.

Ten days later the summer gear was being added to with hat, gloves and a thicker fleece on Beinn Narnain and Beinn Ime, two of our 'local' hills in the Arrochar Alps, as October started to bite with a few snow flurries.

After a few weeks of being stuck on 222 Munros, it was time to put some more miles on the clock and notch up another long-ranger before the curtain fell on another year. The nights were long and dark now, and the days colder, so a nap in the car would become a necessity.

Sgurr a'Mhaoraich is a bulky mountain hidden away in stag central on the undulating road to Kinloch Hourn, near Loch Quoich. It is a near four-hour drive from Glasgow, so finishing after midnight gave me plenty of leeway for a gentle journey. I could take my time and drink in the sights and sounds of a route which had become familiar, the shapes of old friends looming in the darkness on both sides of the road like waymarkers to take my mind off the distance to travel.

On one occasion I was admiring what I thought were the looming slopes of Schiehallion ahead of me when I suddenly snapped out of my reverie. Schiehallion was more than 100 miles away in the opposite direction. I had been driving in a dream-like state for a few seconds and a formation of clouds ahead had taken on the shape of something I wanted to see.

I had no such problems now. I had become attuned to the long drives and coping with lack of sleep, and knew when I had to pull over to freshen up. On this night, I stopped at a layby on the shores of Loch Lochy, under the shadow of the Kilfinnan hills, and succeeded in dropping off for a couple of hours with the soothing metronome of the water assisting the cause.

The road to the little settlement at Kinloch Hourn cuts off from the A82 beyond Invergarry and runs for 22 miles past the Tomdoun Hotel to the lonely farmhouses at the end, squeezing through a barely single-file passage in the final stretches. It is a section that has first-time visitors fear-struck, with a downhill run that has an all too perfect view of the drop to the rocky torrent on the right. In a bad winter, it would be virtually impossible to tackle.

I was stopping short of this last part, aiming to park at the start of a fine path leading up the mountainside, just past the bridge that crosses a slender offshoot of Loch Quoich. The drive along this part of the loch also has its hazards, however, as this two-mile stretch often seems to be the local latrine for every cow in the area. It can truly be said to be a shit road and there are often skid marks outside and inside the car. It can be as treacherous as black – or brown – ice and there is always the added hazard of standing parties of cows on the tarmac.

Sgurr a'Mhaoraich is 'the peak of the shellfish'. Towering over Loch Hourn, the slopes of the mountain were said to be strewn with the remains of molluscs deposited by seabirds fishing in the loch. Standing above the water it looks impregnable, a muscle-bound heavyweight ready to take on all-comers. From further along the road, it is not so tough.

I took the well-engineered stalker's path which starts just beyond the bridge, and goes up in zig-zag sections with a minimum of effort. After crossing the Bac nan Canaichean ridge you come to an impressive dyke running across the ridge. It is a sheltered spot for a break, with the final bastions of the hill dead ahead.

This side does not show the hill at its best, however, and a full traverse is a more satisfying way to do it, curving round from the main summit to the lesser peak of Am Bathaich, with its views of the South Shiel ridge, and then dropping down to the lonely settlement at Alltbeithe and following the shore-side track back to the starting point.

That was the way I had intended to go, but the low cloud that had settled in around 6am never shifted and I was left with a disappointing ascent of zero visibility. The view from the summit on a clear winter's day is magnificent, taking in everything from the Nevis Range to Knoydart and Skye but I was lucky to see even the back of my hand. There was no point in continuing round the circuit; better to cut my losses and come back another day.

Perhaps this feeling of disappointment had also affected the mood of the stag I encountered on the way down. He was standing on the path and showed no sign of moving as I approached. Fair enough, the territory is more his than mine.

The rutting season, when the stags can be aggressive and unpredictable, was almost over. Maybe he had been stood up and just wanted to kick the shit out of whoever was near. I was not in a particularly good mood myself. It was a stand-off between two grumpy old bastards.

I flinched first and gave way, going off the path to take a circuitous route around him before rejoining it further on, all the time keeping an eye on him. After all, I had an old dear to get home to, even if he didn't.

13
Stars and Scones

NOVEMBER IS THE AC/DC month – it can go either way. Some years it can be a bitter forerunner to the onset of winter, other times it is benign – as if it has found contentment in a cosy, wee pub with a roaring fire and cannot be bothered to move on.

Winter was being kept at bay by reasonably warm nights so I felt comfortable enough to head for another nocturnal adventure. What I did not desire, however, was a long journey. It may well be decent weather south of the Highland line, but travel a few time zones further north and the elements could have anything lying in wait.

For example, I keep an eye on the weather forecast for Stornoway because I have friends who live there. It is a pointless exercise, really, because every time you look it seems to be raining. The people of Lewis must have more words for rain than the Eskimos do for snow. It comes in all shades and shapes, wind-assisted, horizontal and vertical. I would not be surprised to hear that it rains upwards, just for variety.

Given the amount of precipitation, you could be forgiven for thinking the place should look like the Amazon rainforest. But no, wind and cold gang up with the rain to keep out the trees.

However, on a favourable day, with the sun shining and the wind taking time off, there is a natural beauty that makes this corner of the world heaven on earth. Like so much of our wonderful country, one lovely day can beat a Mediterranean climate for most of the year.

On this occasion I decided to go for Carn Bhac, a fairly unexciting Munro hidden away up Glen Ey, south of Braemar. It was the only one of the five big hills in this area I had not climbed, so it promised to be a simple night with a minimum of ascent, although it would involve a distance of about 15 miles – perfect for night walking at this time of year.

The road over to Braemar from Glenshee must be one of the bleakest in the country. If the lower part is the Devil's Elbow then the section at its highest point is the Devil's Arsehole. The ski centre and its bare surroundings do not help, but 99 times out of 100 the clouds are down, sitting like squatters, and it is cold and miserable as the wind blasts through.

Further on, through Braemar to Linn of Dee, is Inverey, basically a row of houses by the roadside. One famous former resident was Maggie Gruer, who gave bed and breakfast to passing climbers and walkers in the 1930s. Her homemade oatcakes and thick scones were legendary, and she was a weel-kent face to politicians, playwrights, poets and the climbing fraternity.

I would have welcomed some of Maggie's hot scones as I pulled into the parking area at 3.30am with the lights picking up the wave movements of an icy mist, but all there was on this night was darkness and silence.

On second thoughts, it is maybe just as well there were no scones. Maggie charged the equivalent of 5p for bed and breakfast. If Fergus heard that scones were included for that price while he paid 90p for a caramel slice it might have tipped him over the edge.

I decided to try to grab some sleep, but it was a full moon and, after two hours of tossing, turning and moving seats, I gave up on any idea of rest and prepared for the walk.

The track down Glen Ey starts almost opposite Maggie's house, near a memorial to John Lamont, a Deeside man who become the Astronomer Royal of Bavaria during the 1800s.

Lamont was one of the leading mathematicians and astronomers of his era and mapped out the positions of nearly 80,000 stars. His research into terrestrial magnetism saw him courted by a host of European countries and his handbook on geomagnetism is still in use to this day.

He was awarded diplomas from academies in Belgium, France, Germany and Edinburgh, and showered with honours from all over the world, including one from Bavaria which conferred the title of nobility on him, allowing this local hero to call himself Johann von Lamont.

There is an observatory in California named after him and a university in New York State. His work is recalled by the Apollo space mission, which landed on the Moon in the Sea of Tranquillity at a spot named Lamont, and there is also a mountain on Mars bearing his name. He was a real star.

The way ahead was wide and stony and, with the moonlight illuminating my route, there was no need for a torch. History lurks around every corner here. Tucked away on the left, down a narrow ravine, is the Colonel's Bed, where John Farquharson of Invervey, a freebooter known as the Black Colonel, hid from government troops in 1715. On a favourable, dry day it is worth the diversion to see the colonel's hiding place, a slanting shelf of rock, though in wet conditions it can be slippery and dangerous.

After about an hour-and-a-half on the grey, bone-hard track I found myself at the ruins of Altanour Lodge and its curious, lonely circle of trees, all bent northwards as if they had been caught in a nuclear blast. It is a grand spot for breakfast, with a choice of seating on the huge blocks which have fallen off the building. Ahead lies the massive bulk of Beinn Iutharn Mhor, a hill often known as 'big hell's peak', and the area below is offered in some translations as 'hell's glen'. It was often told that walking down Glen Ey into this panorama was like entering the gates of hell, a cold and forbidding place for travellers.

The wind certainly whips through with a vicious sting and the lack of trees merely enforces this point. The more likely translation for Iutharn Mhor is 'big, sharp-edged hill' but where's the fun in that? Better the devil, you know.

Carn Bhac is less threatening, though, and my journey now took me round to the west, following a disintegrating and then non-existent path up by the Alltan Odhar, the dun-coloured water. Carn Bhac is 'the hill of the peat banks' so I was under no illusions above the nature of the trek which gradually takes you up to the summit ridge.

The peat hags are swarming with wildlife. Once, while picking a way through the quagmire, we disturbed a small owl which was feeding on the ground, well hidden from view, and it flew up in a panic.

There is no such thing as a bad hill, but it is not the most thrilling of tops. Indeed, even the map-makers look as though they could not be bothered to find out which peak was the highest, with some maps not even naming the summit on the long, level plateau.

The cairn was ice-blasted, the icicles tilted as if they were leaning over to salute anybody brave enough to venture up here, and the rocks on the plateau were so heavily rimed that my boots would skid off them at times, throwing me off balance. But, despite the freezing conditions and the lack of excitement generated by the mountain itself, I preferred to be there at that moment than anywhere civilised. The walk up Glen Ey past the old lodge was worth any entrance fee for the therapeutic effect to counter a night in the office.

By the start of February the temperatures were positively balmy, so it was time to fill up the car and head for the far-flung lands again. This time I was going up to Ben Wyvis, the bulky monolith which fills the horizon north of Inverness like an upturned oil tanker, or a beached whale.

A blast up the A9 straight after work saw me parked in a layby across the road from the start of the walk. It was 3am and starting right away would probably see me doing the whole walk in the dark, not something I fancied without knowing what the conditions were like on the summit ridge.

In good weather Ben Wyvis can be a Sunday stroll, and often is for the people of Inverness. Summer weekends see the slopes teeming with walkers. In winter conditions, however, it is prone to avalanche. The plan was to have 40 winks and set off around 6am. I had given my office colleagues the plan.

"You're going to sleep in the car in mid-February? Are you nuts?"

I assumed this was rhetorical, but I took the point. I did not intend to sleep much anyway, I reasoned. A wee nap and the cold would soon force me up and out of the car double quick. I put the seat back and shut my eyes.

The next thing I knew I was being rudely awakened by a huge truck thundering past. It was nearly 7am. I had slept in. For the first and only time I had fallen soundly asleep in the car and it was so warm that my body and brain had obviously combined to keep me there.

This was a heatwave in February. It may have been global warming, but the good news was that there was no chance of bumping into a polar bear up there.

The unseasonably warm climes had not lifted the cloud base much, however, and there was little heat on the long, flat summit ridge where the main cairn had a ring of iced water around it. My new crampons were looking like a waste of money.

However, this is Scotland and, a few days later, it was snowing fiercely. It was like the weather had also overslept, panicked when it saw the time and then arrived at work in a bad mood, determined to remind everyone who was still in charge. For the next few weeks the hills were decked out in white and the hares did not look so foolish in their white coats.

It was April 1 by the time I was back chasing down the remaining mountains on my list of Munros, and the next one would be a biggie.

Deep in Glen Affric are the mighty twins Mam Sodhail and Carn Eighe, and tucked away at the back of them is the Munroist's bete noire, Beinn Fhionnlaidh. It is the hill that sits proudly above Loch Mullardoch, sticking its tongue out at the bagger, a hard-to-reach peak that involves a tough day whichever route is taken.

It also has a ferocious history. Black Findlay was an archer of the Clan McRae, employed by the MacKenzies of Gairloch to police the deer forests on their lands. After an argument, he killed a MacDonald clansman who was trespassing and 12 men were despatched to take their revenge.

Findlay's wife was no slouch in the homicide department, either, and she poisoned all but one of them, most likely with something involving sausages obtained from our canteen. When another dozen were sent after him, Findlay hunted them down before killing them one by one.

He was the McRambo of his day, the screen personas of Stallone, Schwarzenegger and Willis rolled into one. Ironically, after all else failed, he was killed by lethal injection – a needle pushed into his brain by a treacherous doctor as he lay ill.

The easiest way to reach Fhionnlaidh is probably to hire a boat at the dam end of the loch and make a direct assault on its north-east ridge. But, apart from the cost of a solo sail, such an approach can have its own problems. A party we met on the summit one spring day were reluctant to climb back down because of the amount of unstable snow on the narrowing ridge. They faced a long walk round the hill by going down the other side.

Then there is the magnificent overland approach from Iron Lodge, a long walk round from the west that entails the crossing of two or three waters. They can be a real problem in wet weather and it is a long way back.

Most folk just bite the bullet and use the Affric route and I felt I was ready to take it down by circling the three mountains. I had driven there with Space warbling *Mr Psycho*. Were they playing my tune?

Glen Affric is a long, tree-lined stretch with the views improving with each and every twist of the winding road that leads up from the village of Cannich. It is a seriously long drive to get there and by the time I reached the main car park I felt in need of a snooze.

Unlike the February night on the Wyvis expedition, however, it was freezing – making it impossible to sleep. There was only one thing for it: I would have to get moving.

There was a track walk-in which would make life easier for the first hour or so and by the time I hit the path it would be light enough to see my way clearly.

Mam Sodhail and Carn Eighe are huge mountains, bristling with satellite peaks and any day climbing them will be long and almost certainly involve crossing a few extra summits. My route would take me west along the side of Loch Affric, then north-west into the huge Coire Leachavie and up on to the main ridge. The route was still open to debate.

I was starting to warm up as I headed along the track past the lodge, and icy plumes of mist were rising from the loch. When I reached the corrie entrance, the snowline was lower than I had originally thought and it looked deep in the corrie bowl. These conditions could pose a serious problem for gaining access to the ridge and there was always the risk of avalanche.

Instead, I decided on a more direct assault and went straight up the front of An Tudair, one of the outlying peaks. Once on this ridge, I figured it would be an easy enough high-level walk round to Mam Sodhail. It started off as plain sailing, but the higher I rose, the more the icy mist enveloped me and I was soon in full winter conditions, being blasted by a strong wind carrying icy hail which stung as it slapped at my face.

Visibility was now severely limited and the ground was so hard I needed to put on the crampons. I began to suspect that doing three huge mountains in these conditions was a no-no. But, as I neared the final climb to Mam Sodhail, a figure came walking out of the icy mist from the direction in which I was heading.

"Howya doin'?" he asked as if we had just bumped into each other on Sauchiehall Street.

"Have you been up there already?"

"Yeh. I was camping just down the ridge last night. The tent was frozen solid. It took me about an hour to get it folded away."

"What did you use – an axe?"

"Yeh, it's a bit mental isn't it? I'm cutting my losses now, though, and getting out of here."

And with that he walked off. I felt like saluting him as he vanished into the mist, a tribute from one fellow lunatic to another.

Minutes later I reached the summit cairn, a six-foot tall circle of snow and ice-covered rocks that looked more like an igloo. Just below the summit are the remains of an old weather station. It has been unoccupied for many years, its main purpose now being somewhere to shelter from the wind for 10 minutes, even if the snow is piled up inside to the height of the now-vanished roof.

The route on to Carn Eighe goes down into a deep V. It was short but steep and slippy on the ice-blasted path, and the prospect of then losing a lot of height and heading for a mountain that I could not see was beginning to seem too adventurous. Besides which, I doubted I had the time.

I could picture Fhionnlaidh sitting out there mocking me, a look of triumph on its rocky face. It was celebrating April Fool's Day with another notch on its belt.

A week is a long time in Scotland. One day you are battling blizzards at the top of a mountain, one week later you are running round four peaks in shorts and tee-shirt trying to avoid being sunburned. A trip to Glen Shiel gave me both: brilliant sunshine on the way up Gleann

Choinneachain at the foot of Loch Duich, which turned to rain, then blizzards and back to sunshine on A'Ghlas Bheinn and Beinn Fhada.

That was the last hurrah for the northern assault on our weather and, a few days later, any remaining snow had melted away in the blistering heat. An early rise and a three-hour drive saw me heading in to the Fannichs along the banks of the sparkling waters of the Abhainn an Torrain Dubh, on my way to doing a round of four Munros.

I skipped over Beinn Liath Mhor Fannaich, its finest feature probably being the view to An Teallach, then headed over to the highest peak of the range, Sgurr Mor.

As I sat on the summit enjoying a bite of lunch, an elderly gentleman came walking slowly up to the cairn. He told me that this was the first Munro he had climbed, many years ago. He was now in his 80th year and was touring Scotland with his wife, showing her all the peaks and places he had been to as a young man.

I asked if he was planning to do the full round. "The wife is waiting at the foot of the hill in the car," he said. "If I'm not back in 10 hours she'll kill me."

The oppressive heat ushered in thunderstorms which raged with sudden fury over the next few days. Just 24 hours after I had sat on Sgurr Mor talking with the octogenarian Munroist, a walker was killed during a thunder and lightning storm on that same peak.

That summer saw a higher toll of deaths than the winter, and it was the same for the next couple of years. The unpredictable weather and the mix-up of the seasons no doubt contributed to the fatalities but it is also a fact that the vast majority of people who venture into the hills in winter are better prepared, and more knowledgeable about the conditions these days.

Summer in Scotland can be a relative term and the numbers wandering the wild places are vastly greater than in winter. It is too easy to be lulled into a false sense of security. A stunning summer's day at the foot of the hill can be a fight for survival in a blizzard a few thousand feet up.

Two weeks later, a two-day expedition with Fergus polished off the six Ben Alder Munros, broken up by an overnight stay at the popular Culra bothy. We had planned to cycle in the nine miles or so along Loch Ericht and up to Loch Pattack, but this plan came a cropper early on.

I am not a cyclist and the state of the bike I was relying on was not the best. Not long after starting to weave and wobble my way along the lochside track, I nearly mowed down another walker and ended up crashing into a ditch.

"Stuff this, I'm taking the car," I told Fergus, who was trying not to wet himself

He cycled on while I went back, piled my gear into the car and drove right up past Ben Alder Lodge, with a bit of bluffing to the workmen who were camped there during renovation work, and then up the rough track to the pony shed just short of the loch, where I left the car.

The white garrions, a hardy breed of ponies which roam around the local landscape until called into use for the stalking season, are known to chew off car wing mirrors but I thought that would be a small price to pay. My trek overland to the bothy was now a much better prospect.

After dumping our gear and booking a bed space German-style by plonking down our bedrolls, we were off to the first of the day's four Munros, Carn Dearg. The red, heathery slopes of this peak can be hard going, but you start with such a height advantage that the torture is soon over and you are on the ridge which connects four Munros.

The next one along is Geal Charn, a vast, muscled mountain which throws up some impressive cliffs as you head along the path. Then it is just a case of locating the cairn on the vast, flat plateau. This may sound simple and in good, clear weather it is, but in thick conditions and with snow and ice hiding the path, it can be tricky. It is also a good test of navigational skills to find your way down through the cliffs when coming along the ridge the opposite way.

In contrast, a short descent and then a beautifully tapered ridgeline takes you on to Aonach Beag, the little ridge, in little more than 30 minutes and then another short, sharp pull brings you to the fourth peak of the day, Beinn Eibhinn, 'the delightful mountain', and its views down the length of Loch Ossian which likely give it its name. By the time we had dropped down to the pass it was getting late so, instead of tackling the other two hills over the way, we walked to the bothy.

Low cloud and a gloomy sky greeted us next day as we dragged ourselves out of the shelter and headed up the Long Leachas, a spiked ridge which rises up in rocky stages from the banks of the river, and which needs a bit of handwork before you can reach the summit plateau of Ben Alder.

'The mountain of the rock water' looks like it could have been a peak of classic shape that was dropped from a great height causing it to splatter all over the countryside like a giant pancake. The summit plateau, which covers a huge area and has very few points of reference in foul conditions, is ringed with a grand array of cliffs. And it is the scene of an intriguing mystery.

A man's body was found in a sitting position at the edge of a cliff face, overlooking a little lochan. He had been shot in the heart with an old-fashioned lead bullet. He had a waterproof jacket and a sleeping bag but was wearing ordinary slip-on shoes. All the labels had been cut off his clothes and all forms of identification such as bank or credit cards were missing. He was carrying a small sum of money and a replica Remington antique pistol lay at his side.

Police deduced that his clothes came mostly from French stores and about a year later, after an appeal involving a facial reconstruction, he was identified as Emmanuel Caillet, a French student. He had come to Britain a year earlier and sold his car for a knockdown price. His family had not heard from him for nearly two years.

It was discovered that he had stayed at a hotel in Glasgow and his identity was confirmed. His death was put down as suicide, but there are still many unanswered questions.

One witness said he thought he saw the victim with another man at the remote Corrour railway station to the south of the mountain. Some forensics experts have questioned whether it was possible for Emmanuel to have shot himself because of the position of the body and the powder marks on his clothes.

There were rumours that he had been involved in fantasy war gaming and that this role play had been acted out with other people. His parents hired a private detective, but the case has still never been satisfactorily explained.

The Ben Alder plateau is a lonely place to die and there have been a few accidents here. The main part of our navigation down to the col involved avoiding the huge cliffs on the left as you head over to Beinn Bheoil, a feat we managed despite not being able to see a thing.

It is a quick pull up to the summit over the subsidiary peak of Sron Coire na h-Iolaire, with a superb view down the length of Loch Ericht. Unfortunately, it was hidden on this occasion, and we beat a hasty retreat back to the bothy to pick up the rest of our gear and head for the car. It was nice to find my wing mirrors had not been eaten after all, and we were soon back at the railway station at Dalwhinnie before heading home.

The only confusion regarding this outing was a female colleague who mistakenly thought Ben Alder was a friend of mine, an error which came to light when she asked for Ben's phone number in case she needed to get in contact with me. But Ben was ex-directory.

14
No Food, No Trousers

I WAS NOW STANDING at 241 Munros down, 43 to go. I was still on target to finish before the end of the 1990s, but it would mean getting into some of the remotest parts of the country and some very long, tough days. I still had the notorious Fisherfield Six to climb, and I had not yet managed to venture into Knoydart.

Knoydart is revered by walkers and climbers, a Valhalla for lovers of the outdoors. The peninsula on the west coast of Scotland sits in a kind of limbo between heaven and hell, thought to be a reference to the two sea lochs which flank it north and south – Loch Hourn (heaven) and Loch Nevis (hell).

It is home to three magnificent Munros and every one is a hard-fought prize. There are only a handful of inhabitants, no roads or motor access and limited accommodation.

The way in is via a small ferry from Mallaig to the south, or by foot from the east. The latter involves a big pack and a stay of at least two nights.

The most famous route in from the east is the Barrisdale Path, a six-mile yomp along the shores of Loch Hourn to the bothy with a degree of ascent and effort that often catches out the unprepared. If you continue on over the pass leading to the main settlement of Inverie, and Scotland's remotest pub, The Old Forge, you will have covered about 15 miles over tough terrain.

The other three routes in from this direction are equally daunting. The Knoydart area has the highest rainfall in the country. Rivers and streams can quickly become impassable and the few bridges are occasionally washed away.

Only once have I been travelling there when a bridge was down, and even then there had been advance warning, and we were able to cross the river much higher up.

Put a group of walkers together who are planning an expedition into this area and you will soon hear the horror stories surrounding the Abhainn Cosaidh, one of the rivers that pour down an ever-tightening corridor to empty into Loch Quoich. My mates and I have long referred to it jokingly as the River of Death, but it would be no laughing matter if you were faced with the prospect of trying to cross it in wet conditions.

One stunning, hot summer morning, I boulder-hopped across without batting an eyelid, while en route to climb Ben Aden. When I reached the other side I looked back and noticed the watermark on the grassy banks, about three feet above my head. With heavy rain hammering down and water running from the steep slopes and walls all around into the rushing torrent, it must be an awesome sight.

The chance to finally lose my Knoydart virginity arose when I discovered my climbing club was heading there for a weekend early in July 1998.

It had been about a month since my last big hill trip. Work had been busy with Scotland taking part in the World Cup in France, where games were played virtually every evening. Almost inevitably it ended in disaster, a 3-0 humping from Morocco sending us homeward to think again. It would be nice to have a few days away as a nation mourned.

The plan was to walk in by the Barrisdale Path late on the Friday night to reach the slightly more upmarket bunkhouse known as the White House.

About a dozen of us left Dundee at 6pm in a minibus that had seen better days and, after a brief stop at the Tomdoun Hotel for some of the old guard to have a few stiffeners for the march ahead, we reached the end of the road around 10.30pm.

The midges were out in force as we set off in single file with head torches blazing. From across the water we must have looked like a massive, glowing caterpillar wriggling along the shoreline.

I travel light, so my rucksack was not a big expedition bag. It was fine for a winter's day on the hills or a brief overnight stay, but not a three-day expedition. Rather than buy a huge new rucksack, I decided instead to take the two smaller ones I had.

As the night unfolded I was soon to learn that this was a bad idea. It is hard enough walking along a rough path through thick vegetation with only the light of the moon on the loch and a head torch for illumination. With one heavy sack on my back and another one on my front, I was walking like a pregnant duck. It is amazing the amount of stumbling you can fit into a two-and-a half-hour walk.

Although it was dry there was a lot of moisture on the vegetation, and the waist-deep and sometimes head-high grasses and ferns were taking a toll on our clothing. We were cursing the continual foliage showers and wishing that we had had the sense to put on our waterproof gear earlier. But feeling wet was a better option than being feasted on by clouds of midges, who love a standing target, so we pressed on without stopping.

Eventually we reached Barrisdale Bay, the still waters backlit by the moon and all the little islets popping up as black interruptions on the glassy floor. The White House has the luxury of bunk beds and rubber mattresses, a far cry from the bare boards in the other bothy, a few hundred yards back along the track.

It was after 1am, and there was minimal unpacking, as everyone wanted to hit the hay. Stripping off my wet outer gear was the furthest I explored that night. The shock of my poor preparation would not hit home until next morning.

There is no doubt where I acquired my packing skills. In my late teens, I had the typical teenage bust-up with my dad and decided to leave home in a hurry. I had nowhere to go, so I spent that night resting in a giant concrete pipe on a building site and then wandered up to the top of The Law, the hill in the centre of Dundee, to watch the sunrise. When I think of that night now, it was almost inevitable I would one day end up wandering round the high places of Scotland during the wee small hours.

The next day I checked in at a hotel for a couple of nights until I could find a flat, and my mum arranged to have a suitcase of my belongings dropped off there.

The case weighed a ton – I could hardly move it, never mind lift it. When I asked what she had packed, her reply was: "Just the things you'll need and some things to remind you of home."

These included 20 or so long-playing records, tins of food and a giant, stuffed red frog which took up half the case. Not much in the way of clothes or necessities. And it wasn't even my frog.

It's a pity she had not thought to pack our large, box record-player, so that at least I could have been listening to Canned Heat's Bullfrog Blues while I booted the large, grinning amphibian around my hotel room in a fury, decked out in the only pair of undies I had. And to whittle away the hours for the rest of the night I had the prospect of trying to chew my way into a can of soup, thanks to the lack of a tin opener.

When I opened my bags at the White House, I realised my mother's packing skills were hereditary. The last-minute rush had resulted in a worrying lack of equipment. Sure, I had all my safety gear and my sleeping bag, but there was a distinct lack of food. My supplies consisted of a couple of power bars and some nuts and fruit – nothing that I could put on a stove for a slap-up meal when we returned from long walks in the mountains.

Worse than that, I had no spare trousers. Oh well, so long as it didn't rain I would probably be all right.

After a light breakfast, we were ready for the first day's adventure. With the cloud down to around 1,500 feet and unlikely to lift, some of the older hands decided they would stay low-level. The other half of the group were there to knock off Munros, however, and the prospect of a day spent in mist on the high tops was not going to scupper that ambition.

We headed up to the pass, the Mam Barrisdale, from where we would climb the two Munros, Luinne Bheinn and Meall Buidhe.

Luinne Bheinn is often referred to as Loony Ven by walkers and with the wind whipping up and the drizzle creeping into every part of our clothes, it was probably an apt name for the latest loonies to venture up. The real meaning of the hill is more obscure. Take your pick from 'the hill of anger', 'mirth' or 'melody' or, more likely, 'the sea-swelling mountain', another leviathan thought to resemble a towering wave.

The view from any of the Knoydart Munros is spectacular, the sense of space and isolation from the summits supreme. It is a long way back to anywhere from here. We were going to spend the day in cold, windy and damp conditions, and it was going to be a long one.

The ridge that drops off from Luinne Bheinn twists and turns for more than an hour-and-a-half until it finally reaches the summit of Meall Buidhe, 'the yellow lump'. It is hard to see why it would be viewed as yellow, but the fact that the mountain across the glen, Beinn Bhuidhe, is also a yellow hill suggests it may have been a fertile place at one time, and that is the colour the locals grazing their cattle would have seen in the light of spring and summer.

The route is complex, necessitating a lot of compass readings and map checking. Going off track here would add hours to the day.

Eventually we reached the twin summits of our second hill. Wisdom says that if you are doing these hills as a circuit from the pass then the surest way back in bad weather is to retrace your steps, with all the reclaiming that entails. We didn't fancy that and instead dropped down steeply into the Choire Odhair, with its complex terrain providing plenty to think about.

It seemed to take ages battling through thick heather, chest-high ferns and rocky outcrops, but we stuck to our reading and eventually we were back at the head of the pass, just a couple of miles from the White House. Half an hour later downhill and we were stripping off our wet gear and heading for a much-needed cup of tea.

For me, of course, this meant being reduced to a tee shirt, a fleece and a pair of cycling shorts. It also meant being banished to the bedroom like a naughty child. With mixed company, I could not lounge around with just a thin piece of Lycra keeping my carrot and two onions in check. The snugness of the shorts meant I was acutely aware that I was showing more than the gold medallion boys with their Speedos on any Mediterranean beach.

No, I spent the rest of the evening and night upstairs on my bunk, while the rest of the party, trousers all present and correct, mingled downstairs.

My colleagues did try to persuade me to join them. After all, it wouldn't be the first time someone was wandering around in the White House without trousers. Just ask Hillary Clinton. But I felt happier knowing that everything was safely tucked away, and in my bunk I stayed.

The next morning, with the landscape looking like it was wearing a giant, grey beanie hat, we decided it would be wiser to leave the magnificent Ladhar Bheinn for another day. It would be a big walk in grey and damp conditions, and then we would still have the huge trek out. My nearly-dry trousers agreed heartily.

The long, leisurely stroll along the Barrisdale Path was a fine way to end the weekend. It was dry(ish) at this level and the visibility, non-existent higher up, was perfect along the shoreline. I had not managed to do the three peaks as planned but, on the plus side, it meant I would have to make another trip in to Knoydart soon.

There was one unwanted souvenir from Knoydart, however. I may have been fasting on just a handful of fruit and nuts during my stay, but the midges certainly had not. On our annual trip up Buachaille Etive Mor, three days later, I was wearing shorts and, with red lumps covering both legs, my companions thought I had chickenpox or measles. Not quite – it was the legacy of a weekend with a few million hungry midges.

For those brave souls still wearing shorts in the Scottish hills, the Barrisdale Path is probably the tipping point. Apart from the midges lying in wait, the high, damp ferns are a breeding ground for ticks.

The one time I can remember collecting a tick was on Bidean nam Bian in Glen Coe. I came through a thick growth of vegetation and noticed a little, black spot attached to my hand. I hadn't owned a pet since childhood, so I thought I would hang on to him for a while. I called him Tock.

There are many methods of removing ticks – tweezers, talcum powder, playing anything by James Blunt – but the one not now recommended is the old method of burning them off.

"Aye, hold a lit cigarette to their rear end and they'll soon let go."

Hold a flame to the backside of 99.99999 per cent of any creatures on this planet and they will release their grip, screaming in agony. The exceptions, of course, being some members of the House of Lords, who would pay extra for this service.

Anyway, there was no need for bad music or setting fire to anyone's backside, as Tock disappeared of his own volition just after I climbed down some particularly abrasive rock.

Work and holidays combined to keep me off the hills for the next six weeks and, when I did finally have the chance to venture out again, it was to help out a friend. Ellen was heading out to the Caribbean and the yachting life, but first she was going to move all her gear down to her mother's house in Penrith. We decided to set off at midnight to catch a farewell mountain down there, the last chance to climb a hill together for who knew how long.

A greasy fry-up with all the works at 3am in a motorway service station is not the best preparation for a climb, or indeed for your body's future wellbeing. It is remarkable how you can have the willpower to reach the toughest summits in the worst of weathers but not to resist a heart-attack breakfast while a fruit platter option sits just inches away. The usual porridge ritual was right out the window – it was fat-filled arteries all the way.

We started at Glenridding around 5am with the sun coming up, and walked up Striding Edge to the summit of Helvellyn. We even rescued a sheep which had rolled on to its back and become stuck. Then it was down Swirral Edge to Catseye Cam and back to the car still in brilliant sunshine.

By now, there were hundreds of walkers heading up but we were the only ones heading the other way. No-one asked if we had just done the mountain, though.

The car park was also mobbed, and every vehicle had a business card shoved under its windscreen wipers. This is not uncommon, but the message on the card certainly was.

The local gigolo was advertising his escort services and at reasonable rates, too. It gave a name, contact number and the promise of discretion.

Incredulity was the only response, although maybe Ellen's laughter was just a little too convincing. Maybe she was really regretting that she was about to leave the country just as this bargain offer dropped.

I love the far north of Scotland, the empty lands of Sutherland. The peaks here have a true individuality, each with its own remarkable, unmistakeable shape. There are no long, grassy slopes, instead you are faced with weathered sandstone, disintegrating slopes and sculpted, rocky summits.

The two Munros of Assynt, Ben More Assynt and Conival, are a superb expedition but they are a long, long way from Glasgow. I left at 10pm and drove off like Buzz Lightyear to Ullapool and beyond. This time however, the journey seemed a step too far. By the time I had reached the Ledmore Junction, four hours later, a few miles short of my start point at Inchnadamph, I desperately needed to rest.

I dropped off almost immediately then woke up two hours later, wondering where I was. On the plus side, I suppose it's good training for whenever I decide to become an alcoholic.

I set off up the side of the river in an eerie half-light, the track and then well-cut path lending itself well to sleepwalking. About halfway up there is a series of deep caves, the openings to an extensive system of underground passages much explored by caving clubs. I took a peek. It was like looking into a barrel of tar. I would not be venturing any further. I've seen The Descent.

Just beyond the caves, what looks like a giant landslide blocks the way ahead. Closer inspection reveals a path winding up to the col before taking a hard right and then the final push along a soft ridge of peat to Conival, the adjoining hill, the first Munro of the day. There was no sun but it was warm and the visibility was superb, even if the overriding colour was grey. Loch Assynt was shimmering off to the north-west; from this angle its shape made it look like a watery map of the United Kingdom.

The route continues along a ridge of sharp, shattered quartzite rocks to Ben More Assynt, a mountain made up mainly of Lewisian gneiss, one of the oldest rocks in Europe. Ben More resembles a hill in the early stages of demolition. Three cairns sit side-by-side on the summit, broken piles of white rock on bigger piles of white rocks.

When you reach this point, the mountain suddenly becomes Ben No More Ascent. Unless, that is, you fancy a bit of excitement by heading out to the mountain's South Top, which lies one kilometre along the ridge, the traverse involving the crossing of some awkward, sloping slabs. I had tasted enough excitement and exercise, and decided to head back the way I had come.

I had started off in a grey half-light and finished seven hours later in a full grey light. The sky was grey, the water was grey, the rocks were grey. But it was a beautiful day, as only a Scottish grey day can be.

It was grey again a week later when I set off from the Coire Dubh Mor car park in Glen Torridon. The September mist was clinging on down by the roadside as I headed round to climb Beinn Eighe via the magnificent Coire Mhic Fhearchair.

Beinn Eighe is not so much a mountain, more a mini-mountain range, with its two Munro peaks, four Munro Tops and even a Corbett. Its sheer size and scale sees the character of the mountain change on several occasions during the traverse of the ridges.

Then there is Coire Mhic Fhearchair, one of Scotland's natural wonders. A long, rising path curves round the side of the mountain and then pushes up into its heart, bringing into view the magnificent triple buttress towering over the lochain. It must be the best picnic spot in the world.

On this day, however, the mist had stuck with me all the way, and the midges were out in force, which meant getting dressed while walking smartly up the path. Even when I reached the corrie there was no view. I had met several other walkers heading down because of the lack of visibility.

I refused to go back, though, determined that this mist was going to blow away; in any case, I was not going to let a little cloud spoil my chance of another two Munros after such a long journey. I pushed across the corrie floor, gently rising as the path twisted up through the boulder-strewn terrain, until I reached the scree run that leads to the summit ridge of Ruadh-Stac Mor.

Even as I pulled my way up on to the ridge, the mist was keeping pace, as if it had attached itself to my belt, giving no glimpse of what was ahead or behind. I was beginning to think I was destined for another grey-out of a day when, with just a few hundred metres to the summit pile, I burst up through the cloud. It was amazing – one of the most complete inversions I had ever seen. Only the very highest summits were in a brilliant blue sky above the white line. Nothing else could be seen.

Ruadh-Stac Mor, 'the big red peak', was just ahead now in full view, its blinding, white quartzite cap of rocks almost making a mockery of the English translation. For the rest of the day, and the ridge, I was in bright sunshine, while the mist clung on below.

By the time I reached the second Munro summit, Spidean Coire nan Clach, the cotton-wool blanket seemed to have risen again and I could just make out a lone figure reaching the trig point a few hundred feet below me. Then he turned – and vanished. I have always hoped that this stranger knew he was not at the summit and had just chosen to go down. I hate the thought that someone had made so much effort, when so many turned back, only to reach what he thought was the top – failing to notice the higher point further on.

My day was not finished yet. I pushed on along the ridge to take in the peaks of Sgurr Ban and Sgurr nan Fhir Duibhe, with its regiment of soldiers, the Black Carls, standing guard along the ridge.

By the time I reached the road it was dark, so I headed a few miles round to the Coire Mhic Nobuil car park for a bite to eat and a sleep, before a super-early assault on Beinn Alligin, 'the jewelled mountain', a hotbed of myth and legend.

Having learned my midge lesson from the day before, I was fully kitted out for action by the time I swung my legs out of the steamed-up car at 4am and, within two hours, I was on the spectacular summit of Tom na Gruagaich, taking in the hazy views of Liathach and Beinn Eighe.

The heat was stifling, but the views kept on coming as I made my way round to Sgurr Mhor, the second Munro, passing the Eag Dhubh, which slices through the front of the mountain.

Its full name is Eag Dhubh na h-Eigheachd and it means 'black notch of the wailing', a name given by shepherds who would constantly hear cries from the area. They stopped one night after one of the souls who looked after his flock went to investigate, and fell to his death.

The corrie below, Toll a'Mhadaidh Mor, is 'the big hollow of the wolf' and is said to be where one of the last wolves in Scotland was tracked down and slaughtered with its cubs. On the other side of the mountain is Loch Toll nam Biast, 'the loch of the hollow of the beast', where a kelpie, a supernatural water-horse, was often heard bellowing from under the ice sheet of the waters. Kelpies used their cries to lure humans, particularly children, to the water, in order to drown them and then eat their victims. They had the power to transform themselves into beautiful women, but they stayed cold as death to the touch. Most guys have known a woman like that. Usually they are from Edinburgh.

The mountain has one more piece of excitement for walkers, the Horns of Alligin, three summits consisting of piled pancake rocks with all sorts of levels of scrambling available. It is a wonderful conclusion to a fine mountain.

By the time I had circuited and was heading down, there were lots of other walkers out in force. And the midges were there to greet them.

15
Anatomy Lessons

IT IS OBVIOUS WHY mountaineering was once considered to be a man's game – just look at the identification of the hills. Why are so many mountains in Scotland named after breasts? It can only be the work of men.

Sgurr na Ciche is a conical-shaped hill and translates as 'peak of the breast'. Its neighbour, Garbh Chioch Mhor, means 'rough peak of the breast'. Mamores? Paps? See what's happening? Do you think whoever named these hills had a fixation?

If it had been left to the ladies I'm sure there would have been more poetic, romantic names, but boys will be boys and it is not a real sport unless there's a knob gag involved. The biggest of them all is in the Cairngorms.

The Devil's Point is a cleaned-up version of the original Bod an Deamhain, the Penis of the Demon. Legend has it that the local ghillie, being too embarrassed to reveal its true name to Queen Victoria when asked to do so, presented her majesty with a different version.

Cac Carn Beag, the main summit heap of Lochnagar, is safer in its Gaelic version rather than 'little pile of shit', and don't get me started on An Coileachan, the 'little cock'.

Undoubtedly the Gaelic, Celtic and Norse monikers for our hills make them sound more romantic. If they had English names, all the Beinn Deargs would simply be Red Hills, Carn Gorms the Blue Hills and Buidhes the Yellow Hills. They tended to be named locally, the inhabitants of the glen seeing them as big hill, middle hill and little hill for identification in their own little kingdom. The fact that the next glen could have identically named hills proves the point.

Sometimes the names reflect the colours of the vegetation or the light on different hills, other times they reflect a dramatic event that occurred there. Stob na Broige in Glen Coe, for instance, is 'the peak of the shoe', possibly because someone lost footwear there in the distant past.

Some folk are never happy. One recent suggestion was that Scottish hill names should be changed so that each had a unique identity. The logic is that it would make life simpler for rescue teams and helicopters searching for lost climbers if there was only one Carn Dearg, instead of 10.

Is that not what map references are for? Maybe climbers should be barred from the hills if they share the same name as someone else. We can't have the RAF rappelling down to pluck John Smith from a sun lounger in his garden in Aberdeen while another John Smith is lying in the Cairngorms with a broken leg awaiting help.

On a freezing mid-November night I was back on the road to hell, along the side of Loch Arkaig.

If it is not a good road in summer, in the dark of winter it can be downright spooky. The woods on either side of the road are thick and, in places, no light penetrates. Every so often there is habitation of some sort, often with the rusting or cannibalised remains of cars lying around in the long grass. At the back of your mind is the thought that it might not be just vehicles that are devoured here.

On this night-time drive I half expected to see a terrified, partly-clad young woman running into the beam of my headlights. It is the perfect setting for a film about stranded travellers being picked off one by one – The Hills Have Ayes.

Heightening the feeling of vulnerability, the end of the road is a lonely place made more inhospitable by the wind whipping along the loch at a vicious lick, rocking the car as you try to summon up the courage to step outside. And outside, the wrath of nature seems to find you no matter where you try to shelter, cutting through all layers, straight into the bone.

However, the hostile location is also the start of so many fabulous walks and, as I left the car at 7am, kitted out and ready to go, for once there was hardly a breath of wind. The sky over the snow-capped Corryhully peaks was lit with a pink glow and all around me the vegetation was rimed with white.

The stone and then grass track that takes you past the house at Glendessary and then the newer lodge at Upper Glendessary was dry but solid and, after about an hour, I left the path to head up the south ridge of the first hill of the day, Sgurr nan Coireachan, on steps punched out of grassy stopes.

The view from the snowy summit was fabulous, as the name 'peak of the corries' would suggest, low light in the direction I had come from providing a touch of menace while, in the other direction, the rising sun showed off the peaks ahead as a landscape of light and shadow.

The route down the bone-hard clipped grass and rock surface to the col was slippery and needed care, but I managed to keep my footing and was soon at the start of the long ridge of Garbh Choich Mor.

Along here you are accompanied by a huge drystane wall on your right, as beautifully constructed as Hadrian's Wall, a boundary to keep out intruders. On occasion the barrier seems like the only thing preventing you from plunging down into the chaotic boulder field of Coire nan Gall.

A look back along the crest from the summit reveals the giant rocky python you have ascended. It is always a spectacular sight, but in snow it surpasses itself. The wall continues down to the next gap, the Feadan na Ciche. Feadan means whistle or chanter, an apt name when the wind shrieks through from either side. From here, the summit of Sgurr na Ciche is about 20 minutes away on a couple of switchback ramps through the crags and boulder fields.

Sgurr na Ciche is a gateway to Knoydart, and the peaks and bays of that remote peninsula come into view uninterrupted from the cairn, with Skye and the Black Cuillin rearing up along the horizon beyond. The route now backtracks to the Feadan and the path down past the little stream into Coire na Ciche. From there, a grass ramp leads across the side of Garbh Choich Mhor and then picks up the inward route. Simple enough in summer, but I had not allowed for the severe temperature in the gully. The water was frozen, the rocks on either side covered in thick ice. It was going to be a slow and careful descent, with ice axe and crampons to the rescue.

Eventually I was clear of the problems but, by the time I was back at the car, I was two hours overdue for a safety check and there was no phone reception. My safety instructions had been left with a colleague who did not do mountains, and I knew he would be starting to panic. Sure enough, when I finally extracted myself from cannibal country and rejoined the main road, my phone call found him in a spin, wondering what he should do next. I was in a better state than he was when I entered the office to start my shift. The great outdoors really is good for you.

My tally now stood at 252 and I was well on target to wrap up the Munros in 1999. But I still had December of 1998 to go and planned to add a few more to help the cause.

I had my eyes on two remote mountains in the lower end of the Cairngorms. Carn an Fhidhleir and An Sgarsoch are tucked away, far up Glen Geldie between the Feshie and Tarf rivers.

From any direction it is a 25-mile round trip, a long day, but most of the distance is on a track and would make for fast walking. I estimated 10 hours but, even if I was overdue, it would be a simple task to walk with a torch back to the car.

A 6.30am start from the Linn of Dee car park in darkness and I was at White Bridge within an hour. Then it was on past the ruined Geldie Lodge and the track along by the Geldie Burn to the crossing point – and the first snag of the day. Although the weather was benign for the time of year, the waters were flowing fast and the crossing would be wet. I decided that rather than have my feet soaking wet at this early stage I would keep going upstream to find another way over.

Eventually I did, but I had come away from the track and was now fighting through peat bogs and thick heather, obstacles which were slowing me down. After a weary ascent of the north ridge I was on the flat summit of Carn an Fhidhleir. It means 'hill of the fiddler' but how you would manage to stand in the wind up here to play a stringed instrument is beyond me. It is also one of the few Munros that Munro himself did not summit. He climbed the hill but could not find the highest point. That must have been a real downer.

The route on to An Sgarsoch follows the south ridge then a left turn picks up a faint path to the cairn. Even more unbelievably, this summit was the venue for a cattle market in ancient times. It seems a long way to come to buy or sell a cow, but then it does lie on the boundaries of three counties and was probably regarded as neutral territory.

I was running late so, rather than take the route back north to the track, I thought I would try to speed things along with a circuit by dropping east to follow the Bynack Burn to the ruins of Bynack Lodge. My mobile phone battery was dying, so this would be the last chance to call home to let Alison know my new route and head off any concern when I did not turn up until later. It was like trying to explain algebra to a moose.

I rattled off where I was and where I was going. There was a baffled silence and then she said: "Let me go and get a pen."

"Nooooo! Come back – the phone will be dead by the time …"

"Right, I'm here. Where are you?"

I told her again as slowly as I could with phonetic spellings.

"Wait a minute. Ach, this pen's not working. That's one of those cheap ones you bought – I told you they were rubbish. I'll need to get another one."

And then she was gone. The phone had given up, probably in frustration. If ever there was a moment for hill rage, this was it. The next small furry or feathered creature that crossed my path was getting it. I descended the slopes in a fury.

Second snag of the day. By the time I was down at river level it was pitch dark. Still, I was fine if I could find the ruins of Bynack Lodge. And I would have, had it been a proper ruin and not just a ring of stones overgrown with moss and grass, invisible even in daylight. By the time I had worked this out I had lost the slim chance of making the river crossing in any kind of light. The head torch was now on as I approached the river.

Third snag of the day. Remember how I could not get across the smaller crossing on the way in? This one was much wider and, from the roar of the water as I approached, much faster. I knew there was a Land Rover crossing, so logic said the river could not be deep. On the other hand, it was the meeting of two big waters flowing into the Dee, so it could be dangerous.

I stood on the bank shining my torch into the dark waters. I could not see the other side of the river or how deep it was, only how fast it was running. The alternative was a massive detour back upstream which, in pathless terrain and in darkness, was not an appealing option. There was no choice: I would have to take my chances in the water.

The first step into the river was a shock. It was freezing. The next step was even worse: the water was up to my ankles already.

There was no point in hanging around so, with walking poles planted, I stormed on into the river. The water kept rising and soon it was up to my knees, then my thighs. I was tensed for the next freezing upward surge. My big fear was that I would stumble and be dragged downstream by the force of the rush.

How far away was the other side? How much deeper was the river? These questions would be answered in the next couple of seconds: the water did not get any deeper; the next step was back down to my knees, and then I could see the other side. Success – a few more steps and I was out. For a few seconds I was elated – then I remembered that I was at least an hour-and-a-half from the car, was soaked up to my mid thighs and it was December. And icy. There was no chance of drying off.

By the time I reached the car, I was shivering. I could not get my boots off because the straps of my gaiters had frozen to them. It was a cold and miserable run home but, after 12 hours out in the wilds and my scrape trying to cross the river, I felt I had escaped lightly.

It was April the following year before I was back hunting down the names on my list, but I had not been lying idle for four months. Time and opportunity had restricted my movements, so my winter fitness was kept up with a few jaunts to my local, Glen Doll, and the snowy delights of Mayar and Driesh.

There was also time to take in a few smaller peaks and to do a spot of winter skills out in Arrochar. Robert had joined me for a jaunt up Ben Vorlich, ostensibly to practise ice-axe arrest, and the weather certainly did not let us down. Deep snow from virtually the start of the walk, plus iced slopes much higher up provided the ideal conditions.

We were having great fun deliberately falling down the hill, travelling a good distance before the serrated edge of the axe sawed its way into the ground to put on the brake. Unfortunately, though, Robert got it slightly wrong on his next slip. He did not seem to be slowing much at first and made the mistake of pulling his axe out and trying to replant it. That sent him into a spin and he tumbled over and over with the axe pinned beneath him.

When I caught up with him he said his wrist was a bit sore but, otherwise, he seemed none the worse. We decided that was enough adventure for the day and started to head for the car. And just at that moment, I fell for real.

"Thought you said we were finished," I heard him yell, but his voice faded as I hurtled down the steep snow slope. I was travelling at a fair speed, but my axe was in and I did not panic. Just as I was heading for another drop-off, it bit completely and brought me to a halt with my feet dangling over the edge. I looked down to discover that the drop would only have been 12 feet into deep snow, but I didn't know that as I was hurtling down and waiting for the axe to do its job.

"See, that's how you do it," I shouted back up at him, more in relief than one-upmanship.

Robert drove us back to Glasgow but his wrist was starting to swell and, a few hours later, he was sent to hospital. It turned out the fall had broken his wrist.

The good news for him was five weeks off work. The bad news? He had to face his missus. I did not feel like being collateral damage in any marital fall-out, so I decided I had better get back on the road and go somewhere far away.

16
Paras Hilton

THE FISHERFIELD MOUNTAINS in Wester Ross present the Munroist with a series of problems. There were six mighty peaks to be ticked here (one has since been demoted), but to do them all in one round is a serious undertaking. For a start, there is a walk-in of up to two hours with a height loss built in just to reach Shenavall bothy, the base for any six-pronged assault, and of course a two-hour walk-out again at the end.

There is an unbridged river, possibly two, to cross and in wet weather they can bring any expedition to a sudden halt. The Strath na Sealga is notoriously difficult to breach except in dry conditions and even then your feet will suffer. Indeed, the likelihood is that more than your toes will get wet. In spate, only the foolhardy would attempt to cross.

I have been lucky – in three expeditions in here the crossings have not been a major problem. I was completely soaked once, but that was because my boulder-hopping skills were not up to scratch. And it was in the middle of a heatwave, so the ducking was almost pleasant.

One of my former colleagues, however, was not so fortunate. He walked in overnight and stayed at the bothy. A thunderstorm duly hammered down and by first light it still had not let up. When he ventured out the front door he did not get far – he could not see any land. The river had swollen and flooded for miles around, forcing a hasty retreat.

You can break down these six mountains into three epic trips, taking on two Munros at a time. This is certainly my preference as it allows you to acquire a feel for the territory, with all three treks taking a different route in.

However, Fergus and I were men on a mission, and we were going to do all six in one go. This feat would involve an overnight stay in Shenavall and a middle-of-the-night start on the hills. Success would leave me with fewer than 20 Munros to complete.

We set off at 2pm and arrived at our starting point around six o'clock. Twenty minutes later, and with bulging packs, we were heading up the track in Corrie Hallie. The weather was warm and settled, which meant carrying a lot more gear. In winter, you tend to wear most of your clothes and equipment. In Scottish summer conditions, however, you have to be prepared for all eventualities. This would not be a lightweight expedition.

The track leads through the sparsely-wooded Gleann Chaorachain and into an open plain, then takes a diagonal line up and through a bog-and-rock studded moorland. After a while, the path splits and we went to the right, eventually dropping down to Shenavall.

The first sighting of this bothy brings to mind films about the Wild West, a lonely outpost ready to welcome travellers from the hostile countryside. It is a popular destination for walkers, which is hardly surprising, given that it is the only shelter for miles. Even when you make the lonely crossing of the barren landscape in deepest winter, you will usually find some souls have beaten you there. In high summer it can make the teeming streets of Mumbai seem spacious.

There were bodies inside and outside, wandering around, cooking food and generally coming and going from walks on the surrounding hills. There were also tents scattered around, a reliable indicator that it was going to be crowded. We could only hope our rooms had been reserved.

Downstairs offered no joy, with bodies and gear covering every square inch of whatever floor and wall space was available. We climbed the stairs into the attic and managed to clear enough room for our sleeping bags. It was going to be head-to-toe. If you had peeled off the roof, it would have opened a tin of human sardines.

There was even a squad of soldiers, there as part of a charity push to do all the Munros in one continuous round. We were at the Fisherfield Hilton with the Paras.

It was close to bedlam. Our nearest neighbour engaged us in conversation. He was small and bearded with gold-rimmed glasses, behind which his wild-eyed expression hinted at a man on the edge. It was difficult to understand what he was saying. He was either fully tanked or had spent too many unsuccessful days looking for gold in the Fisherfield wilderness.

The night was shaping up to be a long one. Then, after about 10 minutes and the downing of seemingly gallons of water, he began to make sense.

He had tackled the Big Six, just as we planned to do the next day. But he had also tacked on a couple of Munro Tops on the Mullach ridge, a detour of about 40 minutes out and the same back. It was only when he had made the return journey he discovered he had left some of his gear on the furthest peak, Sgurr Dubh. So off he went again, retracing his steps from where he had come, with all the re-ascent that involved. By the time he had finished the full round he was probably on the hills in stifling heat for about 12 hours and was severely dehydrated. It was a stark warning of what we could be facing.

His equilibrium restored, he uttered not another peep all night. Unfortunately the same could not be said for the local wildlife. The rodent population had seemingly descended on this human trashcan with the prospects of a free feast and all night long there was the sound of scurrying, scratching and scraping as rucksacks were raided for a late-night snack. I am certain some of the small creatures were snoring.

You do not find such frenzied activity at any ordinary Hilton. You would call ahead to reserve rodents to gnaw through your luggage – and be charged £20 extra.

It was almost a relief to rise with the light at 3.30am. After a very light breakfast – who can eat at that time of the morning? – we stripped down the packs to what we needed for the day and left the residue at Shenavall, for collection on the way out.

The first task was to cross the notorious water obstacle, the Abhainn Strath na Sealga, and for this we had a secret weapon. Three cheers for our Drywalkers. We had recently bought these simply-made waders after a recommendation from a climbing friend and they were a source of much merriment in the office.

Drywalkers are heavy-duty green bin bags with a sealed-on sole and ties round the knees and ankles, which fit right over your boots and trousers. They make you look a complete idiot, but they are fast and effective, and we were over a notorious stretch of water in moments without getting a drop of water on us. A minute to fold them away and we were off to tackle the first mountain of the day, Beinn a'Chlaimheidh.

The narrowness of its crest may account for its name, 'the mountain of the sword,' but the more romantic version involves a tale of a sword being thrown into a nearby loch as a peace offering after a land dispute between two warring clans was settled.

Going up from this direction is a slow and picky operation, winding through bands of crags and thick heather. Once on the summit ridge, the views are sublime, opening up on all sides, and the whole day was laid out in front of us.

The next hill along is Sgurr Ban, 'the white peak', so named because of the massive jumble of pale, quartzite boulders which crown its peak. It is a long pull from Beinn a'Chlaimheidh and once you start up Sgurr Ban, it is a case of dodging to and fro over and through the massive, often mobile, blocks – some the size of small cars – until you reach the cairn.

Two down, four to go. So far, so good, but we were taking in a lot of fluid and, after a long dry spell, there was not much running water on the route.

A steep, loose scree path leads on to the highest point of the day, Mullach Coire Mhic Fhearchair. 'The peak of the son of Farquhar's corrie' is named after the son of the Earl of Ross, a great hunter in these parts in the 13th century, and it is the highest point on the round. An equally steep scree descent then drops you into the gap between numbers three and four.

Beinn Tarsuinn was next up, the fourth summit of the round, 'the transverse mountain', a crossing point on the ridge.

As we plodded up the stony path we heard the sound of rolling stones, that distinctive clacking you hear when the sea washes rocks up and down the beach. We turned round. Behind us, heading down the Mullach at a great rate of knots, were the Paras team. The first of the four soon caught up with us. They were travelling light, but next came a guy with a massive backpack and then, bringing up the rear and struggling slightly, the fourth member of the team.

When we hit the summit of Tarsuinn, the soldiers were taking a lunch break. They were midway through a continuous round of the Munros, a tour that would take them nearly three months. If the two runners were fit, the one carrying all the gear was super fit. The struggler was the medic. He alternated with two other doctors on the trip, one going out every third day while the two runners and the packman were there every step of the way. This doc must have drawn the short straw.

The next part of the round was going to be the acid test. After a walk down the Tarsuinn ridge over the curious, flat, grassy platform known as Table Mountain, we would have to lose a lot of height before starting to climb another 1,500 feet to A'Mhaighdean.

Physically it is tough to drop so much height at that stage of the day, but psychologically it is even harder. We had been going for about six hours and faced a two-mile drag across the boggy wastes to the slopes rising chaotically ahead of us. We were also low on fluid and were beginning to feel the effects. It was not a pleasurable climb.

A'Mhaighdean is 'the maiden' or 'the virgin', but not for reasons you might suspect. Highlanders called the last sheaf of corn to be cut at harvest 'the maiden' and the mountain's profile from the west apparently has the profile of a bound batch of corn. I prefer to think of it as a young woman defending her virtue from hairy men trying to climb up her sides. Either way, she was putting up a good fight.

By the time we reached the summit there was no sign of the Paras, and we were on our last legs. We still had one last mountain to climb and I was beginning to think that the plan to pick up our gear and then walk out to the car was too ambitious, and that I might be spending another night in the sardine tin. I had to find water soon or risk turning into the gibbering man from Shenavall. Fergus was faring slightly better, but I suspect talking nonsense was not far away for him, either.

The drop down to the pass provided a lifeline. For the first time since we left the bothy there was running water, a small waterfall bleeding out of the side of A'Mhaighdean like a cut artery. We filled every container we had and, after drinking the lot and then refilling them, we were off to the final peak of the day. Within about 10 minutes the water had done the trick – we were back in business.

If we had just deflowered 'the maiden', we were now intent on breaching the defences of her not-so-virtuous pal across the way. The route to the shattered red sandstone bastion of Ruadh Stac Mor appears blocked by rings of crags, but there is a path winding up through the layers of rock. And there it was. After about eight hours we had knocked off the Big Six. Now all we had to do was walk out the 12 miles to the car.

We dropped down the long north-west ridge to pick up the

stalkers' path to swing past the three lochains and follow the route down into Gleann na Muice Beag. This meant a double river crossing, but the Drywalkers came into play again and anyway, we were now too tired to worry about wet feet.

By the time we hit the bothy to pick up the remainder of our packs – just what we did not need at that point, more gear to carry – we had been walking for 12 hours. With the extra weight on our backs and a steady climb back up from the bothy, it was a slow slog up on to the moorland path.

A little more than two hours later we were at the cars and, by midnight, I was home.

Just before I retired for a few days' rest, I threw my boots into the garage in disgust. Fisherfield's 14-and-a-half-hour round had been too much. I vowed there and then I was finished with the hills. The boots would go in the bin the next day.

It was the first time I had ever come off the hills feeling like that. We had struck it lucky with the weather and made it round without injury or mishap, but the mammoth effort had taken its toll physically and psychologically. I lay on the couch for a couple of days, lacking the will to move. My leg muscles were stiff, my body sore all over. Every little task seemed to be gargantuan, an assault on my senses. I was drinking constantly but still could not take aboard enough fluid. I was ramming down food like I had been deprived of nourishment for weeks. I believed it would be a long time before my body forgave and forgot this episode.

However, a couple of weeks later, the pain had worn off and my mind had phased out such bad memories. There was only a good feeling for what I had achieved and the happy, smiling pictures from our expedition sparked me back into life. I started to plan the final assault on my remaining Munros. It was early June and there were still seven months in which to climb the last 18 on the list. I had survived Fisherfield and there seemed few obstacles in the way to the full set. An early-morning jaunt up to the Fannichs took care of Sgurr Breac and A'Chailleach, and my eyes were on the two most northerly Munros, Ben Klibreck and Ben Hope. But before all of that, there was the first outing of the new office mountain club, a venture that would play a huge role in my future hill exploits.

Six of us made the first expedition, a weekend in Lochaber which took in the Carn Mor Dearg Arete route on to Ben Nevis. There was not a soul in sight as we made our way along the linking ridge from Carn Mor Dearg to Nevis in damp conditions, but as we headed down the tourist path there they were: Zulus, sir, thousands of them. The skyline was filled with people of all shapes and sizes in every type of clothing and every type of footwear. It was the start of the Three Peaks challenge – 24 hours to climb the highest peaks in each of Scotland, England and Wales – and we were glad to be heading in the opposite direction.

Six days later, I left home on a beautiful evening around 8.30pm heading up the A9 for the wilds of Sutherland again. It is a long drive, but a superb experience, the light staying with me as I finally cut away from the moonlit waters of the coast and drove inland through Lairg.

The village has the appearance of a frontier post, a final concession to civilisation before you hit the single-track wilderness roads, but it also has a genteel feel. It would not look out of place in the central belt of Scotland. It also has a superb chip shop.

From there it was on to Altnaharra, passing the lonely Crask Inn, sitting on the edge of the moor and, for all intents and purposes, the world. Altnaharra has become synonymous with record low temperatures. You would expect the hamlet to boast bunting and signs in celebration of being the Alaska of Scotland, but it takes time to get things done around here. They had better hurry before global warming melts the local icecap, and the chance of a merchandising bonanza is gone.

Now the road really does become primitive, degenerating into little more than a farm track up Strath More, its scattering of ancient brochs dotting the landscape like old stone beehives. The daddy of them all is Dun Dornaigil and this was to be my spot for a couple of hours' sleep before my charge up the most northerly Munro.

Ben Hope means 'mountain of the bay' from the Norse word 'hop'. Viking invaders have provided many of the names of the mountains in the far north. Suilven, Canisp and Breabag conjure up romantic images of large, bearded warriors striding ashore from their crafts having braved the long sea journey in search of new lands to plunder. Just don't think of all the blood and guts spilled.

There are longer routes up Ben Hope, but my mission was all about speed and I was on the summit in just over 90 minutes going up the direct way, a series of stepped rises. After all, I still had Klibreck to do as well. The view north from the trig point at the top was glorious, the northern coast of Scotland in benign mood, a calm, red-tinted sea with the sky above it striped in pastel shades.

I was back down to the car before the cockerels had crowed and I sat in total silence enjoying a light breakfast before heading down the road for part two of this northern excursion.

Klibreck suffers in comparison to its more northerly neighbour, but it is still a good hill. The Norsemen also had a hand in naming this Munro, focusing on the steep northern slope, the 'speckled cliff' of the title.

It is always hard psychologically to start from zero again after having been at 3,000 feet and I needed a moment or two before setting off from my parking spot near Vagastie, over the grassy terrain to little Loch nan Eun. From there it was a patient and sweaty climb up on to the ridge before an easy push to the summit. If anything, the view was now hazier than from Ben Hope, but it still had its moments.

It was now around midday, but there was still no sign of the rush-hour traffic. I was in no hurry. The journey home was punctuated by several power-nap breaks and it was a full 24 hours by the time I was back to base.

Only 14 to go now and six months left to do them.

17
I Think I Ran Over an Otter

I CAN UNDERSTAND WHY some people feel the need to turn to drink and drugs but it seems a lot of money and misery to try to get high. If you really want hallucinations, all you have to do is work a full day, drive for three or four hours, climb a few mountains for six or seven hours then drive back again and go to work. The experience is free and keeps you fit.

Your mind starts to go, but it is a small price to pay. Your body, on the other hand, puts up a much better fight. The exhaustion you endure is a good feeling of tiredness. I have never failed to sleep well after a night on the hills.

Like the aftermath of drink and drugs, you often wake up wondering what the hell you did the night before. Trying to make sense of some of my earlier diary ramblings is almost impossible. For instance, after a 19-hour round trip to climb Ladhar Bheinn in Knoydart, one of my scribbles says simply: I think I ran over an otter.

I have no recollection of this event whatsoever. I left Glasgow just after midnight, but most of the first two hours of any journey north were virtually on auto-pilot so, by the time I had reached my destination, I had little memory of my drive there. I remember hearing the Cranberries singing *Zombie* and thinking someone, somewhere was taking the mickey; I recall reaching the road end at Kinloch Hourn around 4.30am, setting off from the car on the Barrisdale Path at 5am before first light and then going up and round Ladhar Bheinn and back via Barrisdale to return to my starting point 12 hours later.

I am much more organised these days. Every trip is fully noted with dates, times, weather, conditions and a full account of what happened, who I met and which local wildlife I have killed along the way. I wish I had been as assiduous when I started to compile a log.

Vagueness about some of my nocturnal assaults on the Munros was to the fore during three huge days I spent on an expedition during the latter half of 1999.

I had hoped to finish the Munros before the end of 1990s and, by late July, I had only 13 left. There was much travelling to do, however, and some of the walks were huge, but having done Fisherfield and Skye, I was feeling confident. I had reckoned without exhaustion finally calling to claim back its time.

My working days were long and becoming longer, sometimes 15 hours at a stretch, and the pressures of the job seemed to be mounting. However, I still felt more than capable of completing 13 hills in the last five months of the year.

First up was Seana Bhraigh, one of the most remote Munros. The challenge meant a drive to Ullapool after finishing work and then a seven or eight-hour trek in and out from the south.

A timely reminder about the perils of the great outdoors had been spelled out that day, when 21 people were killed after being engulfed by flash floods while exploring a mountain canyon in Austria. We were in the middle of a long spell of fine weather, so there was unlikely to be any problem in that respect, but one of the difficulties of walking in darkness is that simple routes can become confusing.

A forestry track leads in from the road at Lael, but there are numerous arteries branching off the main route and in the dark I missed the turn-off and ended up heading on the fine stalkers' path to Beinn Dearg. I realised my mistake quickly, but rather than go back to the cut-off I had missed – I hate having to retrace my steps – I decided to head straight uphill, still in darkness, through a steep bank of heather and huge boulders. It was further up than I had realised and much harder work.

Now doubly tired before I had really got going, I was not in a good mood. Thank heavens for auto-pilot. I may have been asleep on my feet but at least my feet knew where to sleepwalk.

Once I was back on track I followed the path to the waters of the Allt Gleann a'Mhadaidh and boulder-hopped across without getting my feet wet. Or, at least, I assumed I did. It can be a formidable obstacle but with the spell of hot, dry weather I had not been aware of it. Either the water was really low or my sleepwalking skills were far in excess of expectation.

So, on a subsequent visit, I was surprised to hear a distant roaring, the sound of Niagara Falls, as I approached. It never occurred to me this could be the same river. The stepping stones were nowhere to be seen and any thought of wading into the water was madness.

Now, with the water behind me and the path starting to snake its way gently up over the moorland, the morning light was shaking off its reluctance to put in an appearance. By the time I had crossed the river and headed past the string of pearls which masquerade as lochs up on the plateau, everything was bathed in yellow. The views were stunning. Behind me, mighty An Teallach, 'the forge', was all yellows and reds as the rising sun set its serrated skyline alight.

Soon I was sitting on the summit enjoying breakfast with cloud inversions all around me and some wild goats looking for a sandwich. Seana Bhraigh means 'old height' and, with the cloud sheet underneath and the brilliant sunlight above, the whole mountain vista took on the appearance of an old, bleached-out photograph.

The sleepwalking took over for the trek back. I remember nothing about it, and needed to sleep in the car before I could even contemplate heading off back down the road to start work. Just 13 to go.

Two weeks later, and I was on the road to Kinloch Hourn. I had failed to do Ladhar Bheinn last time out in Knoydart because of horrendous weather and a lack of trousers, but this time the conditions looked perfect and I was trousered up to the max.

The main difficulty was that tackling the hill from the end of the road meant going in, and coming back out, on the Barrisdale Path. Such an approach necessitated a 12-hour walk, hard enough in its own right but more demanding still when it involved driving to and from Glasgow and not catching any sleep.

The day had been stunning, highlighted by a solar eclipse mid-morning, the first visible in Scotland since 1927. If you believe in omens, then it was going to be a cracking night out.

The Barrisdale Path is one of the most beautiful walks in the country and I would have the pleasure of doing it twice in one day.

Even when you are tired, you tend to keep the pace up. The midges can be particularly horrendous here and any time you stop for a breather, you are immediately under siege.

Once on this path I made the mistake of stopping to change wet socks. Within seconds I was regretting the decision as I fired Skin-So-Soft from a spray bottle at the little rascals with one hand while attempting to remove and fit socks with the other. When my co-ordination became confused by the uneven struggle I sprayed myself in the eyes with the lotion. What a spectacle: a blind man fighting an unseen menace.

It is hard to imagine when following this path that there used to be sizeable settlements along the shoreline at places like Skiary, Runival and Barrisdale. Nowadays there are just a handful of ruins.

Knoydart is a land with a troubled history. It was originally owned by the Clan Donald but, in the 1500s, rights to the land were taken over by MacDonnells of Glengarry. They were partly responsible for forced emigration after the 1745 Rebellion and by the early 1900s the population had fallen from around 1,000 to 600. A famine in 1846 caused by potato blight and the failure of herring catches to reach the settlements around Loch Nevis led to further pain and suffering.

In the 1850s, around 400 people from Airor, Doune, Inverie and Sandaig were driven off by the widow of the clan chief, to be taken away by a government transport ship to America. She wanted the land cleared to increase its value before it was sold to a sheep farmer. The poor souls who stayed behind tried to survive with the little they had left, but most perished during the harsh winter.

Since then the land has changed hands many times. In the 1930s it was owned by Lord Brocket, a Tory MP and Nazi sympathiser, whose intolerable behaviour as landlord led to a famous land raid after the Second World War by the Seven Men of Knoydart.

All ex-servicemen, they seized parcels of land in a bid to break away from the feudal system. The Labour government of the day, however, gave the men who had fought for their country no backing and the Tory admirer of Adolf Hitler won the court battle. It seems that no matter which side runs the country, money and power still trumps the ordinary man.

Brocket sold the estate soon after and it fell into the hands of a succession of businessmen, each of whom had their own plans which never came to fruition. In 1999, after the receivers had stepped in, the community-based Knoydart Foundation bought the estate for £750,000, with a substantial number of donations from all over Britain. The land is now in the hands of those who live there and, consequently, is in a much more stable position, with a brighter future. The biggest challenge is over-commercialisation. Every time I visit the area there seems to be more and more people, and an increase in new building. It would be shame if this bold venture became a victim of its own success after years of struggle.

The first sighting of Ladhar Bheinn from the shoreline path never fails to take the breath away, a fairytale castle with a series of rock spires and towers thrusting skywards as if they were in competition to reach the sun first. Ladhar Bheinn (pronounced *Lar-ven*) is 'the forked mountain'. It can also be taken to mean a hoof and, from this vantage point, it can resemble a huge claw planted in the earth by some massive creature. On a beautiful morning, though, it looked more the realm of princesses than ogres.

A grassy ramp leads down to the head of Barrisdale Bay and then a track follows the shore past the sandbars and the bothy to a small bridge. From here, a path leads across marshy flats and takes you to the foot of what looks like an impenetrable forest of ferns. But a hidden path slants one way and then the next through the waist-high foliage, transporting you to the entrance of the magnificent Coire Dhorcaill. Far below to the right was Barrisdale Bay, thin trails of water snaking their way through the mudflats that had taken over the area for a few hours, and further along was Beinn Sgritheall, the massive scree mountain whose slopes seem to roll down straight into the water.

Entering the corrie gives you another lift. The initial walk along the path keeps you high among a scattering of trees and thick vegetation, before it dips down into the heart of the cauldron.

Now comes the slog up on to the ridge. I have done this on several occasions and every single time it is brutal. Once on the ridge, the angle eases and the route is obvious on a path which follows a roller-coaster line over the steep-sided Stob a' Choire Odhair and then on to the summit.

As I crested one of the peaks, standing in my way was a small roe deer. It was enjoying the rich pickings at the top of the slopes and did not seem keen to move. If there was another way round I would have ceded the ground, but she looked better equipped to deal with the steepness all around and, eventually, she scampered off along a grassy face.

Then miracle of miracles – there were other people on the summit, a couple who had been staying in Knoydart and who had come up from the other side of the mountain. In all my early-morning jaunts I had hardly ever met another soul on the hills. Shepherds, sometimes estate workers or stalkers, but never other walkers.

Having said that, it was nearly lunchtime. I did not mind the intrusion on my mountain because it made a change to see other people, if only because they were able to tell me the time. And no, they were not figments of my imagination although, now I come to think of it, at the time they both looked rather like otters.

If I thought I had escaped my sleeplessness, though, I was mistaken. I kept thinking I saw people who then turned out to be trees. Coire Dhorcaill is a beautiful, atmospheric place but lacks the sounds of animals or birds. Its silence is like walking into a grand cathedral, and it can be eerie.

Clint Eastwood once sang that he talked to the trees "but they don't listen to me". Not only were the trees listening to me, they were talking back. The first time it happened was unnerving. I was convinced someone was calling to me. After stopping to have a look around, I put it down to the wind rustling through the trees and the rocks bumping against each other in the stream hundreds of feet below the path. But the voices kept coming, and every shape became another person to my tired eyes. On several occasions I believed I could see someone ahead of me. That person invariably turned out to be a tree. After a few similar mistakes I started to relax and went with the flow. It was an almost dream-like state, an out-of-body experience and the results were some interesting conversations.

"Hi, there. Oh, you're a tree. Amazing. And how long have you been a tree?"

I could be a member of the royal family, demonstrating the right amount of madness and politeness in equal measure. Anyone coming across me would have been alarmed. I was shambling along, dirty and exhausted, occasionally muttering to myself and my tree friends.

The walk back out along the Barrisdale Path seemed to involve a lot more ascent than I had noticed on the way in but, after 10 hours of walking, what's another 1,000 feet or so to climb? I was in bed by 11pm, and relatively sane by next morning.

Eleven days later I was off on another marathon. This time the major difficulty was the worst road in Scotland, the 22-mile stretch along Loch Arkaig. And the stag shooting season was under way.

If I could be on to the hill before anyone in their right mind was around, I could avoid any restriction – or the chance of being shot.

There are certain options to consider:

1 Find out the location of the stalking and talk to the stalkers to let them know you are there.

2 Stick to the main ridges and stay out of the corries.

3 Take another route.

4 Don't wear a novelty hat with a pair of antlers on it.

I decided on choice four, simply because there was no one around at 2am and I was damned if I was going to let the small matter of a high-powered rifle ruin my plans.

With that in mind, I set off for Sgurr Mor. This adventure necessitates a walk up Glen Dessary, then crossing a high pass into Glen Kingie to pick up a path which would eventually lead to Sgurr Mor, 'the big hill'. When you are in a place that is awash with big mountains you know the one that bears such a title will present a massive challenge.

With the shooters in mind, I decided to run up the pass under cover of darkness and get as far on to the hill as possible before they woke and started blasting away.

I don't normally run, but men with rifles make a persuasive argument and I made it up to the pass and over before it was light. My feet had been slipping and sliding on the wet rock and dew-covered grass as I raced up by the gently dripping waters of the Allt na Feithe, puffing and panting in equal measure.

Sgurr Mor is a great vantage point, with the serried ranks of peaks stacked high in every direction. To the left was Knoydart and beyond that Skye, to the right the wild country between the lochs Arkaig and Quoich. Glen Shiel pulled the eyes to the north and to the south there were all the hills of the Glenfinnan road. If there was a better place to be at this moment, I envy the person who found it.

Onward along the graceful curving ridge lay the Corbett peak of Sgurr an Fhuarain. It looked like a long climb away, but later I found myself wishing I had made the time to go on. Years later, I did and it was well worth the effort.

The route back is over the River Kingie and then up a bog-strewn pass, Feith a Chicheanais, a strength-sapping pull which cuts out a lot of the earlier route, but is hard work. The excellent Kinbreak bothy sits here and I popped in for a look. There was a body upstairs looking dead to the world but probably alive, I hoped. I did not take the trouble to find out, just left him alone to enjoy the rest of his kip.

By the time I reached the car park I was shattered. Running is not good for you. There was an estate manager there, patrolling around, handing out fliers about stalking. Basically he was there to stop walkers going up, if he could, but he was not having much success and, in my case, he was too late anyway.

I can understand the arguments for deer culls and the estate's needs to restrict some movement now and then. But there is never justification for shutting off whole tracts of land. A few polite signs would suffice and most people are understanding, if spoken to in a reasonable manner.

Only once have I experienced a problem with access, an old soldier who obviously hated anyone daring to step on to his land at the Spittal of Glenshee. This little tweed-clad martinet strolled over to block our way and told Fergus, Malcolm and myself in a clipped voice that shooting was taking place and we were denied access. The place is huge – just how bad was their shooting? Were they all graduates of the Dick Cheney School of Marksmanship? But it was late October, the main stalking season, and he volunteered a date when we could come back. We took the moral high ground, rather than the actual high ground, and decided to go elsewhere.

When we returned there a month later, however, he tried the same tactic again. This time he was told that we were going up whether he liked it or not. Three angry climbers with ice axes bristling make a powerful argument.

By comparison, the militiaman back at the car park was not so bad. After we had exchanged fake pleasantries we proceeded to lie to each other. I told him I had been there camping overnight (lie), he said that was no problem (lie), I said I hadn't seen any signs (lie), he said he believed me (lie), I said I didn't fancy his job (true – he was a pompous lackey carrying out the orders to win extra brownie points from the lord of the manor) and then we parted on relatively good terms (probably not true).

There were still four months of the year left and I had only 11 Munros to go. But I had underestimated how much the last three trips had taken out of me. My body was shattered, but so was my mind; I lacked the energy to do anything.

A weekend trip to the Lake District with our climbing club was a bit of break, especially as I did not have to drive. Even with that respite, I could not raise the energy or enthusiasm to push on. Seven weeks went by without even an attempt on a hill and the plan to finish them all by the end of the year was looking dead.

A short jaunt to Arrochar to climb Beinn Narnain near the end of October gave me a lift and, a week later, I was back on the long road north to resume my Munro bid. It was also my chance to climb 'the hill of the bunnet man'.

Yes, Maol Chean-dearg (MCD), the mountain that had helped kick off my obsession seven years ago, was in my sights. Again, though, it was a long journey overnight, up through Inverness and then over by Achnasheen, down past Achnashellach and finally, with all the Achs left behind, I arrived at the small hamlet of Coulags.

Maol Chean-dearg means 'the bald red-headed hill'. With a name like that you can understand why a bunnet was needed. From Coulags, a superb path leads north past the superbly kept Coire Fionnlarich bothy and then to the Clach nan Con-fionn, a huge stone where the legendary warrior Fionn kept his hunting dogs tethered.

It is remarkable how the legend always twists towards heroic figures. It is probable Fionn was a wee, rat-faced ned with a baseball cap, a gold earring and an ASBO, his hounds were Staffies called Tyson and Rocky, and the place covered in dog shit.

A short distance further on, another good path heads west to a high bealach and then a push up through loose rock and scree leads to the beehive summit cairn of MCD.

I would like to tell you that this walk to 'the hill of the bunnet man' was worth waiting for, but the grey sheet that covered everything over 1,500 feet killed any chance of a view and my general weariness made the day one massive slog.

I was running on empty. My time for the walk was respectable, it's just that it seemed to take twice as long as it should have. I knew now that I could not finish these hills this year. I managed only one more climb, a mid-November run up to An Socach in Glenshee for a leg-stretcher. Then I went into hibernation.

Not that it was a peaceful sleep. I was plagued by giant otters wearing Celtic and Rangers colours, demanding to know which school I had attended.

Prince was wrong – I wasn't partying like it was 1999. I was disappointed that I had missed my big finish and now I had to come back for the final push in 2000 with a refreshed frame of mind.

18
Mull of Thin Tyres

NEW YEAR, NEW CENTURY, new me. Okay, so I had failed to reach my target of completing the Munros by the end of 1999, but I was now looking at it from a different perspective. I could take a more leisurely approach to the 10 outstanding hills.

For the first months of 2000, I was out on the hills on average once a week. The office climbing club had grown into a merry band who were prepared to climb a hill before they started work in the late afternoon.

A 7am start and a driving range of around an hour gave us plenty of scope. These days out in the crisp, dry days of January and February felt like a holiday after the mammoth excursions of the previous autumn.

One week we were up to the north in Callander, the next to the south in Scotland's highest village, Wanlockhead. We were in the Ochils and Loch Lomondside, Arrochar and the Trossachs, and I was enjoying the Angus hills and the Cairngorms, with lower hills the extent of my climbing. The fare was varied and it was good for body and soul. There was no pressure, no rush.

Except, of course, there were still 10 Munros to finish off.

Ben More, the only Munro on Mull, is a favourite final hill for many. The only island Munro outside of Skye, it is often kept for last when a party of family and friends can make the relatively easy climb and then head for a yahoo weekend in Tobermory.

Despite being so close to the end of the round, I still had no set plan for a final Munro. I was taking them as they came; whenever an opportunity arose I would go for it.

A few years back I had the idea that it would be good to finish on a peak that translated as 'hill of the rowan'. There are three – two Beinn a'Chaorainns and one Sail Chaorainn – but as it turned out I climbed them all within a few weeks of one another. There was no forward planning. It was Triple-O climbing – opportunity over order – so Mull's highest had no particular romantic appeal of being a fitting final hill, just as I wouldn't have bothered if it had turned out to be No.284 anyway.

I had been discussing my Munro options with Jim, my flatmate who had provided the drop-off and pick-up for my 24-hour circuit a couple of years before. His eyes lit up when I mentioned Mull. He had always wanted to visit Iona, so the idea that we team up again to combine my Ben More climb with an island hop appealed greatly to him.

I floated this proposal around the office, hoping to lure another couple of willing bodies for a grand day out. It would also help with the ferry cost; it is not cheap to take a car across to the islands.

Robert was the only one who bit and so, in mid-April, we set off from Glasgow at 6.30am, heading for the ferry port at Oban. We were in a leisurely mood and, after passing through the metropolis of Crianlarich, we stopped at Tyndrum for breakfast.

In Victorian times Crianlarich was a key travel hub and had two railway stations, an important link for those heading off to the north and west. I've often wondered what overseas tourists make of it. The village is on virtually every direction sign in the centre of Scotland and the unsuspecting must think it is a major city, the centre of the Scottish transport system. I could believe that if you travelled to the ends of the earth there would be a sign with pointers and mileages to New York, Beijing, Moscow, London and … Crianlarich. Visitors must be shocked when they arrive there to find a couple of pubs and hotels with a lot of backpackers wandering around.

You could picture a stunned American tourist asking: "Hey bud, is there a Best Western or Holiday Inn here?"

"Best Western? Nah mate, this is Crianlarich. We don't even have a Shite Western." I should point that one of the hotels changed to a Best Western a few years back, but Crianlarich still ain't New York.

Tyndrum has grown up over the years. Once nothing was open before 9am. But with all the potential early-morning custom from lorry drivers, skiers and hill walkers whizzing by, sleepy hollow had to change. The famous Green Welly Stop now offers two or three different eateries, Paddy's Grill has one of the best value all-you-can-eat brekkies and the chip shop is usually mobbed.

The village has also changed with the influx of a new wave of foreign workers. Poles, Czechs and other eastern Europeans have largely taken over from the Aussies, Kiwis and South Africans who used to staff many of the bars and cafes. It wouldn't surprise me to find the zloty is now an official currency of Tyndrum.

The decision to allow an expansion at the gold mine in nearby Cononish may also see another boom for the settlement. It could be become the Las Vegas of the Highlands, with wild-eyed prospectors stumbling into the local bars to live the high life. When you add the busloads of golden girls that seem to arrive by the minute on their tour buses, it has the potential to become a powderkeg. Some of these 85-year-old predators can be a handful after a few sherries.

Back on the road, I took the turn-off on to the A85 round to Oban. It was at this point that we thought it wise to check the ferry times. We did so, only to be told there were no ferries running to

Mull. The timetable we had looked at the day before was last year's. This year, the summer schedule started three weeks later.

We sat at the side of the road, stunned. Our prospects did not look promising. Then the woman on the phone said: "Of course, you could go from Lochaline."

Her suggestion was positive – but at that point she could have told us to head for Venezuela and it would have sounded better than the impasse we faced. I knew the way to Venezuela, but Lochaline was a complete mystery.

A frantic search of the road map gave us the good – or bad – news. We would have to get back on the A82, follow it all the way up to Corran, just south of Fort William, where we would take a ferry into Ardgour, on the Ardnamurchan peninisula. Once across Loch Linnhe, we had 33 miles to travel to Lochaline. It seemed a bit of a push but we decided to give it a go. Besides, I was driving and although I had a modest Astra, I could still give Jensen Button a run for his money.

Our drive seemed like one of those dashes when every light turns green at the right time. We made it to Corran just before the ferry was set to leave for the five-minute crossing and we were on the other side of Loch Linnhe by 9.20am. Now we had 33 miles to do in 40 minutes. Could we manage it on these roads?

The first 12 miles down to the Strontian turn-off were fast, a clear road with long stretches for overtaking. But we now faced 21 miles on a mostly single-track road. As we hurtled along we met a line of traffic coming the other way. These were the cars and vans that had just disembarked from the ferry we had to catch. It was going to be tight.

We reached the loading area with seconds to spare, even if we had left a lot of tyre tread on the road. For a man who had once been treated to a day out with a professional rally driver, Jim looked a bit pale. He said: "I've never seen driving like that." I'm still not sure if it was a compliment. Robert kept a diplomatic silence.

Fifteen minutes and £26 later we were at Fishnish Pier on the

Isle of Mull. The driving was not so frantic now and we were soon through the little settlement of Salen and at the foot of Ben More on the shores of Loch Keal. The sun was out and sparkling on the water as Robert and I kitted ourselves out and waved farewell to Jim, who was off round the coast to take the little ferry over to Iona. After the frantic rally driving, the peace and quiet of St Columba's Isle would do him good.

Iona is a place everyone should visit at least once. The tiny Hebridean island has been a haven of tranquillity and beauty for thousands of years. Monks, pilgrims, kings and artists have all headed for its shores, looking for inspiration or perhaps just a few days' break.

There is a reverential hush there, as if the peace is transferred in a huge wave to everyone who steps off the boat. Bronze Age mourners buried their dead here and the abbey graveyard is the final resting place of many early Scottish kings. It is where the former Labour leader John Smith lies, a fitting spot for a true political gentleman.

There are better routes up Ben More but this was a smash-and-grab visit. The best views were all behind us so at least we were hopeful of a beautiful walk down. We passed several parties of walkers on the way up and the summit was busy with children and dogs running around.

The sun was shining but there were still snow patches at the top and there was a strong, cold wind. We would not be picnicking here. We took our time coming down with plenty of photo stops, the little isle of Eorsa looking particularly fetching in her new spring ensemble.

By the time we hit the shore there was still no sign of Jim, but the wind we had experienced at the top was non-existent here and the sun was beating down. The rocky beach was a suntrap, so we stripped off the heavier outer gear to take in the rays. When Jim came back along the road about half an hour later, we were in Mediterranean mode and in no mood to move on. But time and ferries wait for no man so we were soon back on the crossing to Lochaline.

Jim was now the driver and he was hanging on to the wheel like grim death. I suspected there was not a chance in hell he would let me drive the single-track section again, so it was a more sedate run back over the 33 miles to catch the Corran ferry.

The laid-back atmosphere continued with a meal and a drink at the Kingshouse and then a second stop at the Ardlui Hotel for more refreshments. The fact that Manchester United were on television, losing their Champions League second leg 3-2 at home to Real Madrid, probably kept us there longer than we intended. The atmosphere was electric and every goal the Spaniards scored was greeted with a deafening cheer.

Big Jim, who was not really into football and the strange culture of wanting teams to lose rather than seeing others win, said: "This is amazing. I didn't realise there would be so many Spanish tourists here at this time of year. It must be a real boost for the local economy."

It was close to 11pm when we arrived back at the flat, 16-and-a-half hours after setting off. They don't make days like that any more.

I have often pondered over how much a round of Munros costs. For a solo walker, petrol costs alone are exorbitant. Our local mountain club, like many others, have had to stop hiring minibuses for weekend trips. The cost has risen so steeply that they cannot be covered by the numbers going. The bus journey was often one of the best parts of the day. It did not really matter where you were heading or who you were with, if you were not driving it was a day out. But if you have to use your own transport, you become choosy: you might as well go somewhere you want to go with someone you would rather be with.

The consequence of rocketing charges is that mountain club memberships have dwindled. Some have amalgamated, some have folded, while the rest plough on with higher costs and fewer bodies to share the burden.

Other factors conspire against the clubs, too. Many sprang up from big companies which subsidised their staff activities, but a lot of these firms have cut back jobs over the years and slashed spending.

Staff subsidies are often the first thing to go.

The reason I started to think about the costs of climbing centred on Ben More. A recent solo trip to Mull set me back about £200. I had travelled from Carnoustie to Oban on a wet and wild Wednesday night in February so that I could catch the first ferry in the morning. Because it was a winter timetable, I had to take the car over on the boat, as the last crossing back was cutting things too fine.

I spent the night at a hostel in Oban, and I had also stopped for a pub meal in Tyndrum. Breakfast would be a CalMac special on the ferry, and I would have a bite to eat on the way back as well.

Totting it all up I was about £60 for fuel, £56 for the ferry ticket, £25 for the overnight stay and around £30 for food and drinks. The total comes to about £170, but there was a sting in the tale.

The country was still reeling from the most severe winter for years and the roads had suffered particularly badly. When I swung the car off the ferry on a gorgeous sunny morning I was only about 25 minutes from the foot of the mountain. But as soon I started driving along the A849, the main coast road along the island, I knew my timings would be out. The situation was horrendous. There were potholes every few yards and the road surface was torn up in huge sections. It was more like a dodgem ride, with drivers sometimes being forced on to the opposite side of the road to avoid the huge craters.

Once or twice I heard a bang and felt the car lift then bump back down after running over a badly broken section. I was dodging the worst bits – so far. About halfway to Salen, I heard a huge thump and felt the car lurching to the right. Then I heard that dreaded clumping sound as the car dragged along, a certain sign that one of the tyres had been shredded.

My heart sank. I had come all this way and been blessed with the weather for a perfect hill day, but now it was more likely I was going to be sitting around waiting for the car to be repaired, sweating over making it back in time for my ferry.

A quick look confirmed the worst. The tyre looked beyond repair.

But one of the benefits of having car trouble on the islands is that anyone passing will almost certainly stop to offer assistance. Within minutes, I was on my way to the garage at Salen courtesy of one of the locals.

The owner of the garage gave me a lift back to my car and changed the wrecked wheel. Then he told me to get on and climb Ben More and he would sort things out.

I knew it would be a costly day out but at least I would have my climb and plenty of time to return to the garage before heading for the ferry.

After four hours and a stress-free ascent, I was back at the garage to face the music. I was expecting a bill of at least £100. Instead, I had to hand over just £30. The tyre was fine, it was just the wheel rim that was damaged and the mechanics had managed to straighten it out and reset the tyre.

I was astonished. I had been at their mercy. They could have fitted a new tyre and I would not have argued. I needed the car fixed. Instead they showed remarkable honesty.

I suppose it is a sign of the times that an act of decency leaves you stunned. Apparently mine was the fourth car that morning that had fallen victim to that particular pothole so maybe the garage owner was rubbing his hands anyway. Nonetheless, it was a breath of fresh air not to be ripped off.

Ben More had set me back £200 but it could have been a lot more, which set me wondering how much the average Munro cost.

So here is the arithmetic, with all figures rounded up and calculated in today's money.

I took 151 days to complete the Munros. At an average travelling distance of 200 miles per trip, total mileage amounts to 30,000.

I was averaging around 40 miles per gallon and, with petrol about £6 per gallon, fuel costs add up to £4,500.

About a third of these trips meant an overnight stay at a rented house, hotel or hostel, so adding an average £25 per night for 50 nights totals £1,250.

Food and drink, including breakfasts on the road, packed lunch, provisions and the occasional meal on the way home – £2,000.

I went through at least 10 pairs of boots, possibly more, at an average of £100 per pair – £1000.

Add £2,500 for all my other gear over the eight years – rucksack, torches, ice axe, crampons, walking poles, waterproof jackets and trousers, fleeces, technical tees, thermals, walking trousers, winter trousers, socks, cycling shorts, gaiters, hats, gloves, sunglasses, miscellaneous items including compass, maps and midge repellent – and you arrive at a grand total of more than £11,000. Excluding the depreciation in the value of the car.

There were 284 Munros, so the average individual cost is approximately £40 per Munro. Ben More, at £160 over budget, was probably the most expensive Munro.

Over the last 20 years I have climbed more than 1,000 peaks and, on these calculations, must have spent upwards of £40,000 ticking names on a list. Still, all the fresh air was free.

Next, it was time to settle an old score. Two years ago, I was forced to turn my back on Beinn Fhionnlaidh, the remote peak far down Glen Affric, on a day of snow and ice storms. Now, on a perfect May day, it was time to go back and conquer it.

The giants of Mam Sodhail and Beinn Eighe would have to be climbed again, but I had not seen them at their best last time, so I had an added incentive.

The contrast could hardly have been greater. Last time out, visibility was zero as I battled my way along the massive ridges while being pelted by shards of ice, nine hours of walking in horrendous conditions which saw me abandon any hope of climbing the elusive Fhionnlaidh.

This time I enjoyed a slow, steady climb up the stalkers' path in Coire Leachavie and then on to the ridge just south of Mam Sodhail, under a blue sky filled with thin wisps of white cloud resembling candy floss that been teased out to its limit.

The huge cairn on the top of the mountain is built in drystane fashion and can be seen from miles away. It was even bigger when it was built in 1848 by a team from the Ordnance Survey, standing at a height of 23 feet with a circumference of 60 feet.

From there I dropped down to the pass and then took a bypass path across the side of Carn Eighe to obtain my first clear view of Beinn Fhionnlaidh. It is not much of a pull-up and a good half-hour yomp took me up to the cairn of the one that got away.

After taking in the expansive views from the top, most walkers are struck by the realisation of the daunting climb that now faces them to reach the top of Carn Eighe.

Mam Sodhail's huge summit cairn resembles a little house on the prairie from this peak, a much sought after location for any potential hermits if they were not put off by the thought of bitter winters.

I varied the descent this time, following the long east ridge over three or four other peaks, including a nice little scramble over some pinnacles, to reach the gap beyond Sron Garbh and its Victorian stone staircase. From there a drop down into the glen and then a path over the river and south over heather-clad ground took me back to the car.

It was second time lucky with Beinn Fhionnlaidh, but the day's walk had taken nearly 10 hours. The Munroist's bete noir does not go down easily.

Just eight to go now and, after a weekend in Glen Shiel with the office climbing club, I was ready for the next assault on my remaining Munros. It was time to take on one of Torridon's finest, mighty Liathach, the huge, dark, forbidding wall that looms over every traveller as they drive down the glen. To the casual observer, Liathach looks impregnable.

There are two Munro peaks on Liathach, Spidean a'Choire Leith and Mullach an Rathain, and they are connected by a pinnacled ridge which requires a lot of care. It is not as tough as it looks at first glance but there are one or two spots that may make the scrambler take a deep breath before proceeding.

The cloud was sitting like a giant grey sponge, just cutting off the tops of all the peaks and squeezing out enough moisture into the air to keep it damp. For a day when it did not rain, I ended up remarkably cold and wet.

My mood had not been improved by climbing about 500 feet up the path from the road before discovering I had left my camera in the car. The steep pull up came as no surprise, with the bonus that you are soon on the ridge, and from there on it is a high-level expedition all the way.

Spidean a'Choire Leith is the perfect place to linger, to look along to the pinnacles on the next section of the ridge, in anticipation – or trepidation. The pinnacles stand in regimented confusion, discoloured and crumbling like a row of rotten teeth, daring the walker to make his next move. But all too soon the challenge is over and I was strolling up to the cairn of Mullach an Rathain and sampling its view out to another Rotten Row, the shattered spires of the Northern Pinnacles.

If the route up is fast, the descent is equally swift, even it does prove a real knee-breaker.

I was staying at Cromasaig, a B&B run by Tom and Liz Forrest at the start of the glen. The location proved to be a real nature watch. No sooner had I climbed into bed when I was aware of something else sharing the room. When I turned on the light something buzzed past my head. Then again, and again. It was a bat and it needed two of us and a bed sheet to catch the creature and put it outside with the rest of its mates.

Next morning I had my first sighting of a pine marten. With sleek, reddy brown fur, a yellow band running down its front and a long, bushy squirrel-like tail, it is a striking animal. But its teeth and claws are even more impressive. Tom told me he had to keep the dogs in when the pine marten was around. Despite its small size it is perfectly capable of shredding a dog's face.

This one was a nursing female and it was stocking up for its kits. It was sitting on the bird table outside the kitchen window, shovelling up anything edible, which did not amuse the usual customers.

I was being treated to a Torridon remake of King Kong in miniature – the mighty ape sitting on the top of the Empire State Building being dive-bombed by an avian airforce intent on bringing it down. The main difference was that Kong survived this version and then vanished into the trees, having hoovered up everything on the table.

The next day saw me knock off the wonderful Slioch, then the not-so-wonderful Fionn Bheinn on the following day. Despite being a boring, grassy trudge ironically it yielded the best views of the trip. And it took a mercifully brief two-and-a-half hours. Now there were just four to go.

19
Mission Accomplished

MMMMM – CHEESECAKE. The next foray was one that would have had Homer Simpson salivating. Bidein a'Choire Sheasgaich, situated in the wilderness above Loch Monar, is phonetically and affectionately known to most walkers as 'Cheesecake'. It does not look like a cheesecake, though, more a choux pastry tower spiralling into the sky.

'The peak of the barren cattle' is an inaccessible Munro along with its partner, Lurg Mhor. Whichever way you tackle these hills, a long, long day with a lot of re-ascent or an overnight stay is inevitable.

Approaching from the north involves taking the track from Craig in Glen Carron into a high pass, the Bhealaich Bhearnais, and then climbing over an additional mountain, Beinn Tharsuinn. Nearly four hours' walking is required before you reach the foot of Sheasgaich. By the time you have gone over it and reached the summit of Lurg Mhor, you are six or seven hours in and have climbed about 5,000 feet. To get out you must retrace your steps or drop north near the head of Loch Monar with a massive loss of height. If you are not super fit, it is a huge undertaking.

Taking on these hills from Attadale or Achintee in the west is not much easier, but there are a couple of good bothies under their slopes which can be used to break the journey and provide much-needed rest.

I decided to tackle them from the north but, instead of having to make the long way out in the same day, I would drop west off the side of Sheasgaich and head for the Bearnais bothy, a couple of miles down the corrie and across the river.

Timing would be everything. As I did not want to be sitting around at a bothy in daylight hours, I would aim to get there for dusk, go straight to sleep and then be up at first light to go out a different route, following a good path over yet another mountain, Sgurr na Fearstaig.

The midges were massing in the wooded car park at Craig as I set off at 1pm, the rain chucking it down and my pack loaded with the extra weight of sleeping bag, roll mat, more food and drink than usual and a change of clothes. It was late August, so I had given myself an eight-hour window to do the three peaks and then drop down to the shelter.

Fifteen minutes later the clouds had dispersed and the forecast sunshine was blazing down. The heat was drying me out fast, the steam rising from my clothes. Fifteen minutes later the heavens opened again and I was sloshing my way along the track heading for the bridge over the river and then, after another 15 minutes, it was roasting again. The weather was stuck on a wash-dry cycle.

This time I ignored the notices to use the two-wire bridge and instead took the more regular wooden one further down. Once over the river, I headed south-west for the pass and the rising ridge of Beinn Tharsuinn. This is a pleasant little hill but to most folk on a Munro mission it is a nuisance. On a day like this, however, with no deadline to get home or back to work, it was a superb warm-up for the main event.

The first sight of Sheasgaich takes the breath away. The north ridge rises steeply and looks intimidating, with rings of crags guarding the route to the summit crown. A closer inspection reveals a steep path of sorts winding its way in and out of little gullies between the rock bands and, with a minimum of handwork, you are soon facing the final push. The summit is a little eyrie with a tiny cairn but it provides an expansive view east down the length of Loch Monar.

In theory, the shores of the loch would provide another fine approach but the reality is a nightmare, a pathless trek through bogs and thick grass for mile after mile. Your boots, and your soul, would be destroyed long before you reached the hills.

It had taken just over five hours to summit Sheasgaich. I left my pack at the col and made the beautiful trudge up to the cairn of Lurg Mhor, 'the big shank', with the glowing light starting to fade for the day. I was tired but satisfied. The plan was beginning to look perfect – even if I had made an early start, I was never keen to drop all that height and then re-climb around 2,000 feet through rough terrain just to get back to the pass.

The backdrop of the evening light as I looked east was making the rocks on the summit shine, but a look back at Sheasgaich showed that night was beginning to stretch its shadow from the west, with only shafts of light breaking through to hit the tiny pools of water in the corrie.

Now I had to move fast to get down to the bothy. My only thought was to get my boots off and lie down, hopefully to slump away into unconsciousness for eight hours, but the steep route down Coire Seasgach was not easy because of wet grass and mud. By the time I was halfway down, the dark had settled in and I had to watch where I was putting my feet.

The downpours which had peppered the day had left a lot of standing water and I could hear the roar of the river ahead in the dark. I would need my waders to cross. But I could also see a light from over the water. Someone was in the bothy. I could only hope it was not a lunatic – there would be no room in this asylum for two of us.

Bearnais is a small bothy but generally not a busy one. I knew there would be room at the inn, but when I tried the door latch, it would not open. I walked round the building. Yes, there was definitely a faint light inside. I went back to try the door again. Locked. I looked in the window. There was someone inside. I banged on the door. Two, three times. Finally, the door opened tentatively and a face peered round. Come on, man, it's unlikely to be somebody trying to sell you double glazing out here.

A German-accented voice said: "Oh sorry. You were wanting in?"

"No, no, just checking you weren't needing any milk delivered."

On entering, I saw why the light was so faint. This fellow and his girlfriend had erected their tent inside the small room and it was taking up virtually all the floor space.

They had thought they would be alone and I had stumbled in to ruin all notions they had of a romantic night under canvas. But I was soaked and tired and not in the mood for any lovey-dovey nonsense. However, Michael and Hanna turned out to be great company. Hanna even made me a cup of hot chocolate because I looked so cold. I was freezing.

Despite the roll mat and the sleeping bag, I did not enjoy good slumber. Lying on bare boards in a cold bothy is not conducive to sleeping well and even with a change of undergarments and socks it still felt damp and miserable. My wet clothes were hanging up, but not drying, and I was tossing and turning all night in the damp air. About 5am I shot out of my bag with muscle-gripping pain in one leg. Cramp. That was the end for me – there was no point in trying to lie down again. Best to get dressed and start out early. But, of course, my boots and all my outer garments, despite hanging up all night, still felt like they had come out of Aquaman's wardrobe.

Putting on damp clothes is one of the worst feelings in the world, and I would have to endure discomfort for another five hours on the walk out.

As it turned out, my suffering was not so bad. The day brightened and after the initial slog uphill, Beinn Fearstaig's undulating, rocky summit ridge with its many tops proved to be a pleasant alternative to the inward route. I reached the car by 1pm, exactly 24 hours after setting out. Even the midges had stopped being annoying.

The next time I climbed these hills I decided to come in from Attadale. Again it involved an overnight stay in a bothy, again I would find two companions there and, again, damp and cramp were the key words.

I usually take different approaches when going round hills for a second or third time, or I climb them in different seasons from the first time. On this latest occasion, it was just as winter was receding for another year that I set off from the car park at the entrance to Attadale Gardens for the six-mile walk-in to the Bendronaig bothy. I would rest there for the night before setting off early in the morning for a circuit of the hills from Loch Calavie in the south.

The track goes round by the gardens and through a wooded stretch with holiday homes dotted around on either side before crossing a bridge and then winding steeply up and into more open ground. I had moved off in fading light and by the time I had got this far it was fully dark and my torch was on.

In total darkness on an overcast night in open country a torch is only good for seeing a couple of steps ahead. Beyond the limited range of the light anything could be lurking. You could easily wander into a flock of sheep or not be aware of someone coming the opposite way until the last minute. So your pace naturally slows.

The hills were still in winter condition and I was wearing the heavier and warmer gear to suit the season. I also had a heavy pack with all the winter accoutrements like crampons and ice axe as well as sleeping bag, roll mat and emergency tent, plus extra food and drink for my night out. Two hours later and I was getting close to my base for the night.

Bendronaig is one of the better-kept bothies. It has a main room with fireplace, tables and chairs and there is plenty of wood for the fire. There are three small rooms off the main one and the wooden floors throughout are in good condition. There is also the luxury of a flushing toilet, although it cannot be used during the winter for fear of water freezing in the pipes. Sitting beside the bothy is the grandly named Bendronaig Lodge, which looks just like a bigger version of the bothy, used for estate management, but at this time of year – and night – it was deserted.

In daylight, the light-coloured buildings can be seen for miles around; in pitch darkness they are invisible until you are within three feet of them.

There was no light coming from the bothy and after a quick inspection of the building – no gear left waiting for return parties – it seemed I would be the sole occupant.

The walk in had been accompanied only by the sound of my footsteps on the loose path and the gently running current of the Black Water. If anyone was going to arrive in the night then I would hear them approach.

The room I chose to sleep in had a fireplace and an old table and chair but, otherwise, was empty. Everything had to be done by torchlight. It was very cold and the temperature seemed to be dropping with every minute.

It is eerie to be alone in total darkness and complete silence. I kept thinking how I would probably have a serious trouser accident if a face suddenly appeared at the window. Combined with the cold, my unease kept me tossing and turning for most of the night.

I must have drifted off because suddenly I was aware of two pale figures standing in front of the fireplace. The man was dressed in a Victorian-style tweed jacket, shirt and tie, plus-fours and something that looked like a deerstalker. The woman had on a Queen Victoria dress and a lace shawl over her head and shoulders. They were having a discussion about land reform.

There seemed nothing strange about this but the conversation came to a sudden halt when a blinding white light of pain flashed in front of my eyes and my right leg muscles tightened with cramp. I leapt out of my sleeping bag and started to ease my leg into circulation. Only then did I notice my two companions had gone.

I have to admit I was unsettled. I decided that I would not try to get any more sleep here tonight.

Subsequent inquiries have failed to explain that weird experience. The consensus is that there are always strange stories emanating from bothies. A friend tells a tale of McCooks Cottage on the Ben Alder estate, a bothy renowned for strange and spooky goings-on. It was said that a ghillie once hanged himself there and there have been umpteen stories from spooked walkers about noises coming from the other room in the middle of the night – sounds like furniture being moved, despite the room being empty.

Opinion seems to be split on this phenomenon. There are many sane and rational people who claim to have seen and heard things, and some refuse to stay there. Others have stayed there without anything going bump in the night.

One of the old guard of my friend's climbing club had been relating a tale of an experience he had there to a gathered audience during one of their weekends away. He was telling of strange sounds and an unsettling aura in the room, describing the growing unease of both he and his friends. He was milking the moment, building up to the part where he hoped everyone was about to jump off their chairs with terror as he delivered the final blow.

"And then from nowhere a packet of McVitie's milk chocolate digestives suddenly flew across the room."

The place fell apart with laughter but he was raging.

"You bastards can laugh if you like but I know what I saw."

September 2000, and it was down to the wire. Two solitary mountains to climb and I could break open the champers. Many people have a big party to celebrate finishing the Munros, with children and relatives all joining in for the last day out. The traditional finish is to have a piper playing at the summit and then a dram or two to mark the occasion.

However, weekends were out for me and most of my climbing colleagues worked weird and wonderful hours, so I would carry on doing my own thing and if anyone could come along, fine.

The other complication was that this was going to be a two-day midweek operation. Day one would see me tackling Maoile Lunndaidh from the Craig approach in Achnashellach, and day two, the final Munro, would be Am Faochagach, a big, featureless mound just south of Ullapool.

In the end, two of my mates were going to make it. Derek and Giles would join me for the second day. It was a long drive from Glasgow to climb one hill, but they insisted they were coming. I would call Derek at work when I had successfully seen off the first Munro, and the pair of them would meet me next morning for the final climb.

Fuel protestors were blocking the oil refineries, but I was all tanked up and ready to go.

Again this would be a late kick-off. Sheer luxury. Like my previous outing to Cheesecake, I started from the car park at Craig just after midday. The wind had picked up further and I was being jostled as I set off up the track in the kind of squally conditions that make you think the rain is heavier than it really is. On the plus side, there were no midges and I would not have to think about crossing the two-wire bridge as I was heading further up on the track towards Glenuaig Lodge.

After about half an hour I met two walkers coming the other way. I asked what they had been doing.

"We're going down mate. The wind is horrendous. You'd have to be mental to go up there." Sounded like an endorsement to me.

Soon I met another party. They had also decided to abandon any plans to go high and were doing a through walk instead. "You'd have to be mental…" Then another group who were heading out with the same mantra.

Where was the sense of adventure? Man against the elements – that was what it was all about. Okay, if you were at the bookies you would place your money on the elements for an away win but still, it couldn't be that bad. By the time I had reached my cut-off point for the mountain, I was beginning to have doubts. All the little streams had broken away from their mother and were running riot. It was like walking on water, a trick that could come in handy later.

Maoile Lunndaidh means 'bare hill of the wet place'. If ever a hill deserved its name this was it. Water was everywhere. The wind was lifting it from the sides of the hills and spraying it all round. It was as if the gods were indulging in a giant water fight and I was the innocent victim caught in the crossfire.

I pushed on south up the right-hand ridge of Maoile Lunndaidh. The wind was blasting in from the west like an express train and it was a case of two steps up, one step back on the steep grass. Then the rain really came on and I struggled to make headway. I felt as if I was walking into the jet of a fire hose. This approach was not going to work. I would be lucky to make the ridge and if the wind was bad here then what it would be like up there?

However, as I crested the ridge, the rain let up and the wind suddenly became my best pal, hanging round my shoulders like a Friday-night drunk. As I turned slightly to the left for the final pull-up, the gusts were right behind and started to push me up. The further I went, the easier it became. I was being blown to the top of the mountain. I even stuck my poles away, spread my arms and let the wind carry me even faster. I had made the summit of my penultimate Munro, and the wind-assisted lift had improved my struggling times. I was back on schedule.

It was dark when I arrived back at the car park so I had a hard job finding my motor among the dripping pines.

My first task was to phone Derek and let him know I had made it. I was a couple of hours overdue and I was lucky to get him, just as he was leaving the office.

"At last. I was beginning to think you hadn't made it. Anyway, well done. So that's you done 276 now then, eh?"

"No, that was No.283."

"I thought there were 277 Munros?"

"There were, but now there are 284. They changed the list a couple of years ago."

All I heard was: "Ah bollocks! Look, got to go. See you tomorrow." And he hung up.

That was strange but I thought no more of it as I headed down to the Aultguish Inn for the night, anticipating a hot bath, a good feed and a warm bed. The room was spartan but even Xerxes' Persian hordes could not have kept me awake that night.

Next morning I had a lazy breakfast and hung around taking in the peace and quiet. For once, it felt like I had all the time in the world. After a couple of hours of outdoor meditation just watching the day come to life, the boys turned up and we headed a few miles up the road to the final starting point.

Am Faochagach was not the best choice for a final Munro. It is a dreary plod over heather-clad and bog-strewn flats up to the ridge and then a long but fairly simple walk to the summit.

You would think my final Munro would have a special place in my heart. But no, I have never felt affection for it and, with each subsequent ascent, I have come to dislike it even more. And this big, dull lump does not even have good views from the summit.

Am Faochagach does have one element that adds spice – Abhainn a'Gharbhrain, the river that guards any access from the south. In very dry conditions you can sometimes boulder hop across without getting wet feet. In normal conditions, and in this part of the country that means wet, it is a trickier prospect – knee deep if you are lucky, waist deep if you are not. In spate, you will probably drown.

Fortunately, this obstacle is only 10 minutes from the start of the walk, so you know early on whether this is the hill for you. Once, when we were heading away from the car park in deep snow to do a round in the Fannichs, another party was leaving the same spot for Am Faochagach.

"They'll be back in 10 minutes," I predicted. They were.

We were somewhere in the middle of the crossing range. It was not raining but yesterday's monsoon had ensured the river was swollen enough to give us a hard time. I had my plastic bag waders, and we could share them.

The water was deep and running fast, but I made it over at one spot where it reached just above my knees. With a boulder in each wader, they were flung across for Derek to use and then the same again for Giles. We would have to do it all again on the way back but getting wet just 10 minutes from the car was hardly a problem.

After the water hazard, it's a push upwards to the ridge on grassy steps and dark, slippery mud with the consistency of porridge. There was hardly any talking, the constant lack of purchase on the greasy surface demanding every ounce of concentration. Surely your final Munro should be more exciting than this?

After an eternity of slipping and sliding uphill, with the wind whipping our faces, we reached the ridge. I was hoping to see the summit from here, a target to give us the extra impetus to charge on, but there was only a series of rounded crests coated in short-clipped vegetation and rock chips with a wide path disappearing onwards. The grassy, featureless terrain of the corrie on the right did not provide much inspiration, either, but it highlighted the huge expanse of wasteland which constituted this mountain. The summit continued to evade our sight as we struggled on along the open ridge, the wind now taking advantage of the lack of shelter to batter us relentlessly.

Then, just over a final low rise, there were the twins cairns adorning the flat, windswept plateau. We were there. The boys stepped back to allow me to reach the summit alone. It was all over.

I then saw why Derek had sounded so strange the night before. He pulled out a poster which read: 284, September 8, 2000, in white lettering set on a black background. He had been leaving the office the night before with the sign reading 277 when I called, forcing him to go back to change the figures.

They also produced a bottle of Chardonnay for a small celebration amid their two-man round of applause. It would have been nice to set up a picnic table and chill out, but the wind was ripping the skin from our faces and retreat seemed a more intelligent option.

There was still the small matter of the river to re-cross and it was here that Giles came into his own.

If he had been around during the glory days of slapstick comedy he would have become a multi-millionaire. We have seen him tumbling down hills with an artistry that only circus clowns could match, falling backwards *up* hills and generally acting like a demented stunt man.

He did not let us down this time, either. Derek and I had already made it across in the same fashion as before, but Giles seemed to doubt the wisdom of our route and went off course, the water gradually spilling over the waders, down his legs until he stumbled further into the depths with the ever-inflating waders making it harder to walk. By the time he steered his way over you would have thought he had been scuba diving. One day the boy is Jacques Tati, the next he is Jacques Cousteau. Genius.

Epilogue
The Honey Badger

SO THAT WAS HOW I became Munroist No.2,433. Almost eight years to the day from my first ascent, I had conquered all 284 peaks.

It had taken 151 outings and the tally was skewed heavily in favour of the spring and summer months. June was my best month with 75, then September with 45. The winter months of December, January, February and March totalled just nine between them. Hardly surprising when you consider that almost half of my mountains were tackled during the night hours. Winter does not lend itself to overnight walking, especially when you are flying solo most of the time. Night-time walking may seem an eccentric idea, but I was not completely crazy. I would never take the chance of needing the assistance of the rescue services because I had found trouble while walking in Arctic conditions in total darkness.

I loaded the dice as much as I could. I picked my days and nights carefully. I chose peaks that had longer approaches, so that I could get so far in to the hill in the dark. I chose hills with good paths up to the summits – you don't want to be struggling up pathless terrain in the dark. I tried not to pick hills which involved going near anyone's house. I know how I would feel if a lone walker appeared in the dark going past my window with a torch at 2am. I tried to pick my weather. Most of the times this strategy worked, but sometimes it went wrong; the fine forecast on TV the night before could arrive late, by which point I was at the foot of a hill. I always hoped for the best but planned for the worst.

Many people ask what it feels like to complete your final Munro. I have to say I felt nothing. I was proud of the achievement and never regretted the experiences, even when I was struggling up hills while everyone else was likely tucked up in a warm bed. But there was no euphoria, no sense that this was the end of a long journey. The overriding feeling was relief because of my glass half-empty outlook. I was just glad I had managed to finish the task I had set myself before I would succumb to some debilitating illness or be run down by a bus. Now it did not matter. I was quite happy for the No.22 bus to do its worst.

Other Munroists feel the same way. Touching the final pile of rocks on the summit brings about the feeling: Is that it? It is the journey to reach that point and the build-up to it that provides the excitement; the actual peak is just that, another peak. After all, you had to see 283 others to conquer this one.

Maybe if I'd had a huge family party on the final summit with 40 or 50 people present it would have felt different. Probably not. Anyway, if I had dragged 40 or 50 people up Am Faochagach they would have likely formed a circle at the summit and stoned me to death.

In a strange way I think Derek and Giles enjoyed the last one more than I did. They were thrilled to be part of the round and I was happy and humbled that they made such an effort to be there. But if I had gone on my own I would have just run up and down No.284 as fast as I could and then driven home to settle down in front of the telly.

My daughters had baked me a cake and decorated it with the

outline of a mountain and the number 284. That was a better feeling than reaching the final cairn.

No, the real triumph in touching down for the final time came from seeing how far I had come – and I don't mean the distance. From being a naive weekend rambler who did not know the basics, I had become a seasoned hill man with the skills to survive and navigate my way through hostile terrain in all weathers.

From a man who thought Coulags was a prisoner-of-war camp, I had become someone with a deep knowledge of his own land. From a dopey looking (relative) youngster in combat jacket and denim shorts, I now looked and acted the part on the hill – I could walk the walk, as well as talk the talk. I had learned so much in those eight years.

I know now that Germans are wary of cows, that you should never, ever buy a car from anyone with a name resembling that of a Native American tribesman and that trees are interesting to talk to when you are on your own. I learned how to throw dogs over raging torrents and that one over-priced piece of baking could destroy a man's soul. I met Brocken Spectres, ghostly Victorians and imaginary otters and felt relaxed in their company.

Most of all, I discovered that I had mental toughness. Every time I went out on the mountains, I knew I would make it to the top. Even when I did not feel 100 per cent, or when I struggled against tiredness or extreme weather, I knew I would get there and back again.

That is one of the reasons my climbing friends called me 'The Honey Badger'. It stemmed from a discussion during one of our trips. Someone mentioned that the honey badger was the toughest animal on the planet, a real badass in the brutal desert conditions of southern Africa. Some of the guys had never heard of it, so we looked it up on YouTube and there was one of the best wildlife films ever. As soon as the lean, mean fighting machine appeared on screen one of the guys said: "God, that's Rowser."

It was the way it loped along with a no-nonsense look in its eyes, covering 50 miles a day and letting nothing stand in its way. And it had a white streak on its head of dark hair. We could have been used as 'Lookalikes' in the columns of Private Eye.

Hopefully, it was not the fact that it was in a permanently foul mood, or that it killed everything in its path. The nickname stuck and has become a standing joke ever since.

No matter how much I try to sell my vision, there will be people who think my activities are irresponsible madness. This story is not a recommendation for anyone else. It's just how it was.

I have undertaken winter skills training and micro navigation courses. I like to think I know what I'm doing. I also have certain rules I follow when I go solo in winter. I may have made some silly decisions early in my mountain days, but I learned. I do not take chances. If someone was interested in doing hills in this fashion then I would help and pass on advice, but I would *never* suggest it was a great idea.

However, it worked for me. The night-time excursions became my way of doing the Munros. It often took a lot of mental strength to finish a hard, 12-hour day in the office and then, when everyone else was saying goodnight and heading home, drive for three hours into the wilds to climb two or three mountains.

Sometimes I did not make it out of the starting blocks. I soon found out that if I went home with the intention of getting four hours' sleep before rising again to make the big journey, it just did not work. When I did manage to get back out I was always more tired having had my brain switched off for a few hours, convinced that it was in for a good night's sleep. And there were times when I was just so exhausted after a hard day at work that I had to forget the adventure altogether and instead go home to sleep.

However, after the first few false starts and several mistakes, I got into my stride and made the night my own. I loved stepping out of the car at 2am or 3am, in the middle of nowhere. The sounds were different, the smells were different, the whole feeling was different. It was like discovering forbidden fruit.

My body adapted as well. When I started out walking in the middle of the night, my internal organs must have thought: "Oh God, not this again. Does this guy never sleep?" But they soon joined in the fun and never really let me down. Maybe in the years ahead I will pay dearly health-wise for the years of nocturnal adventure. Only time will tell if it was all worth it.

There was simply no feeling like the smugness when I arrived back at the office by lunchtime the following day, having had breakfast 3,000 feet under the clouds, to meet colleagues who were pasty-faced and knackered despite having a good night's sleep. One day when I arrived back in a hurry I took the lift up to the first floor. One young woman, who was obviously a bit miffed at having her clear run up from the basement to the second floor interrupted, pointed to a poster on the wall.

It read: Take the stairs every day and in a year you will have climbed a Munro.

I said: "That's okay. I've just done three Munros this morning so I'm fine to take the lift for the next three years."

I returned to the office with a happy tiredness, rather than an irritable fatigue. The challenge made me mellow. It never affected my work, so it never became an issue for anyone else.

My family were often blissfully unaware that I was out on the hills and, in any case, it was at a time I would not have been with them. I felt I could have flown to Paris after work, partied on the Champs Elysees and made it back next day without anyone being aware I had even been out of the country (I once took the train to Edinburgh and had a cup of tea and a Paris bun in Doug's Cafe and no-one was any the wiser).

All I had to do was change out of my mountain gear to go home and it was like nothing had happened.

"Where have you been?"

"I've been out partying with another woman."
"Liar, you've been out on the hills again."

What do you do when you have finished the Munros? Most mountain lovers know the answer to that one: keep going. The night-time forays that took me round the Munros had become so much a part of my walking experience that it was never going to end.

Within days of finishing my round in such a whimpering fanfare, I was out again, this time in Glenshee to do a round of four Munros, and a trip to Braemar with one of my daughters for an easy afternoon hill.

Next up were the Corbetts, the list of mountains over 2,500 feet; the Munros again; the Munro Tops and the Furths – that's the English, Welsh and Irish 3,000 foot peaks – and I would still be heading out into the night to take them on.

Ten years after finishing the Munros, I was still taking off after midnight and climbing hills. The night outings have slowed down in the last couple of years, mainly because of a change in my working circumstances, but I still take the chance to head for the hills during the twilight hours, given the opportunity.

No-one can know what lies ahead. I just hope that I can keep walking as long as possible. You don't have to be climbing hills. There are parts of Scotland I would still love to visit, some amazing through routes that take you across country through the middle of the mountains. So many islands to explore, so many journeys.

I would like to be the 80-year-old I met on Sgurr Mor, making one final climb at that age to revive a lifetime of memories. Who knows – I might even be able to do it in the middle of the night, to sit on high and watch the sun rise for one last time over the mountains before the light dies in my own eyes.

Glossary

A

ABHAINN – river

ACHADH – field

ALLT – steam

AONACH – ridge

ARETE – sharp ridge

B

BAC – bank

BAN – pale, white

BEAG (BEG) – small

BEALACH – mountain pass

BEN / BEINN / BHEINN – mountain

BHREAC / BREAC – speckled

BIDEAN – small pointed top

BIOD – pointed top

BINNEIN – pinnacle, pointed summit

BRAIGH – slope

BRUACH – slope

BUIDHE – yellow

C

CADHA – steep slope, pass

CAIRN / CARN / CHARN – rocky hill

CAISTEAL – castle

CAM – bent, crooked

CEANN – head

CIOCH / CICHE – breast

CLACH – stone

CNOC – knoll

COILLE – wood

COIRE / CHOIRE – corrie, hollow

COL – mountain pass

CREAG – crag

CRUACH – heap, stack

D

DAMH – deer

DEARG – red

DIOLLAID – saddle, pass

DOIRE – copse

DROCHAID – bridge

DRUIM – spine, ridge

DUBH – black

DUN – fort

E

EACH / EICH – horse

EAG – cleft or notch

EAS – waterfall

EILEEN – island

EUN – bird

FEADAN – small valley

F

FADA – long
FIACAIL – tooth
FIONN – fair
FRAOCH – heather
FUAR – cold
FUARAN – spring

G

GABHAR – goat
GAOITH – wind
GARBH – rough, stony
GEAL – white
GEARR – short
GLAS – grey green
GLEN / GLEANN – valley
GORM – blue
GREIGH – herd

I

INBHIR / INVER – river mouth
IOLAIR – eagle
LAIRIG – pass
LEARG – slope
LEAC – stone
LIATH – grey
LOCHAN / LOCHAIN – small lake

M

MAM – breast
MAOL – bare
MEADHOIN – middle
MEALL – lump
MOINE – moss, bog
MONADH – mountain
MOR / MORE / MHOR – big
MULLACH – height, summit

O

ODHAR / ODHAIR – dun-coloured, tawny

R

RUADH – reddish

S

SAIL – heel
SLOC / SLOCHD – hollow
SGOR / SGORR – rocky-topped hill
SGORAN – little rock
SGURR – rocky peak
SMIRR – misty rain
SOCACH – snout
SPIDEAN – high point above corrie
SRON – nose
STAC – conical hill
STOB – peak
STRATH – valley
STUC – steep conical hill
SUIDHE – seat

T

TOLL / THOLL – hollow
TOM – hillock, knoll

U

UAINE – green
UAMH – cave
UISGE – water

V

VANE – middle

Acknowledgements

SOME THINGS ARE JUST meant to be. Moonwalker had been in my head and in my diaries and notes for around ten years before I got round to writing it. But then spending those years working long hours in a newspaper office wasn't conducive to getting it off the ground – the last thing I wanted to do after a 12-hour session of writing and re-writing was start writing again when I got home.

When I first met the BackPage Press boys, Martin Greig and Neil White, we were working Saturday sports shifts together on the now defunct News of the World. On the day we were all leaving the office for the final time, Martin asked what I was going to do next. I said I would probably get round to finally writing Moonwalker. His eyes lit up. He thought it was a fascinating concept and pointed me towards a publisher.

There were a few stops and starts after that, but then just when I was about to go it alone, Martin and Neil decided to take a chance on the book themselves. As I say, some things were just meant to be. My experience with the guys and their knowledge and enthusiasm since then has been nothing short of first class.

A big thank you also to Herald chief sports writer Hugh MacDonald, who made the editing process a joy and to Bob McDevitt, my first prospective publisher, then my agent for a short time and finally a friend and cheerleader for the book all along the line.

Thanks also to the Glasgow Film Crew boys, Ryan Pasi and Craig Burrows, for their sterling work during a night shoot on Beinn a'Ghlo, my tech guru Gary Duncan, for all his work, patience and advice on the Munro Moonwalker website plus Facebook and Twitter, Jim Stewart for improving the quality of my old pictures and Ken Anderson, a constant champion of the book.

I have enjoyed so many mountains and been given so much support by hillwalking friends but it would be impossible to name check them all. But to those who feature in the book, I apologise and thank you in equal measures: Malcolm Hunter (and Scoop), Robert Melvin, Crawford Brown, Rebecca Ricketts, Evelyn Turner, Carol Anderson, Ellen Arnison, Giles Blair, Derek Watson and all those who remain nameless.

And, of course, my great friend Fergus Wyllie, who sadly passed away earlier this year. I think he would have loved reading about my version of some great days, and knowing Fergus, he would no doubt have been quickly penning his version of events.

And last, but not least, to my wife Alison and daughters Claire and Lucy for having put up with all this madness for so many years.

BackPage Press

More information on Alan Rowan including blogs, photos
and hills & guides can be found at: www.munromoonwalker.com
Twitter: @MunroMoonwalker
Facebook: www.facebook.com/MunroMoonwalker

We welcome your feedback on this book and our other titles…
www.twitter.com/BackPagePress
www.facebook.com/BackPagePress
www.youtube.com/backpage2010
www.backpagepress.co.uk